FROM A PATIENT'S VIEW POINT

Published by:
Bizy Enterprises, Inc.
13 Leisure World
Mesa, Arizona 85206

All rights reserved. No part of this book may be reproduced or transmitted in any form or by any means, electronic or mechanical, including photocopying, recording or by and information storage and retrieval system without written permission from the author or publisher.

Copyright 2010
ISBN, first print edition 9780972262156

Bizy Enterprises, Inc retains all rights and ownership to book, From A Patient's View Point; including publishing and distribution of text and photos.

TABLE OF CONTENTS

About The Authors

Introduction

Chapter I: It Can Happen To Anyone	1
Chapter II: Time Stood Still	29
Chapter III: A step Forward In Recovery	39
Chapter IV: Mixing Science With Spirituality	65
Chapter V: In The Grand Scheme Of Things	77
Chapter VI: A New Beginning	97
Chapter VII: My View Point	103

CO AUTHORS: LOUISE AND WILLARD INGRAHAM

Photo taken at a better time before the crisis

ABOUT THE AUTHORS

FROM A PATIENT'S VIEW POINT was co-authored by Louise and Willard Ingraham. Willard held the pen to paper writing a daily journal as well as taking photos through all of Louise's trials during and after her confinement in all three Tri-Cities' hospitals and a care center stay. The book is a reminder that there is more than science and faith that carries one through difficult times.

This is not the first book this couple have written and published. Willard wrote his first book about his service years during World War II, "Farm Boy To Soldier" and then followed up with his families history and genealogy in, "Echos Past, Links To The Mayflower."

Louise wrote her first book, "Sapien's Journey Through Time and Space then followed with "Atlantis, A New View" and then her families history in "The Pioneer Spirit, Minnie, Charley Williams And Family."

All of the above books are available through Bizy Enterprises, Inc. whose address is on the publisher's page.

An interest in writing for Louise and Willard was not a retirement idea but it was a time table that fit. Both had careers in fields of their interest; Willard in electrical with Public Utility Districts serving as department head in Metering and Louise in branch banking and management. Both spent hours in continuing studies through evening college classes during their working years and after retiring. It only seems natural that they would one day turn to writing.

With this book nearly completed they both have turned a serious interest to the universe and life in space which they have pursued in studies over the years and will write about. Louise and Willard are examples of, "there are always new challenges in life to expand the mind."

INTRODUCTION
By: Louise Ingraham

A life threatening crisis entered my life unexpectedly two years ago turning my world upside down. Embedded in my mind to this day is the pain and frustration I had in not being in control of my own body and not knowing the outcome.

I never felt sorry for myself but I did ask how this could have happened to me. Willard, my husband, was with me at all times and through his compassion and strength the bond we have gave me positive thinking even on those days that I seemed to be floating in another time zone. Our pictures are below.

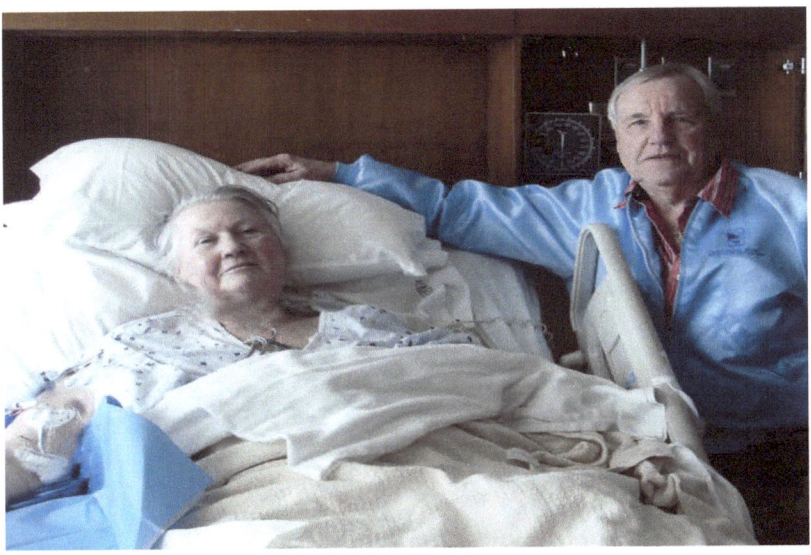

As you read through the chapters of this book you need to know there was a very skilled physician providing his professional services and advice. That person is our family doctor, Dr. Matt Smith. He kept Willard informed and arranged for us to be admitted to the hospital where, as a patient, I would have the best medical attention available for my needs. You can see by the photo, left, that Dr. Smith records his patient's history onto a laptop. I have found over the years that these records Dr. Smith keeps are without a doubt extremely valuable as a reference of my entire medical history for his analysis.

As I look back over a stressful time I remind myself how fortunate I was. There are thousands of others out there that have and are going through life threatening issues in their lives. In many cases the outcomes are final days for these courageous people. I have compassion when I hear or see anyone struggling to overcome difficult situations. Still, vividly in my mind are thoughts of those days I spent in hospitals. It remains difficult to revisit those times so why do I want tell my story?

First and foremost I write because I want to direct more credit to the unsung heroes in my recovery process. One takes for granted that there will be physicians, nurses and other care givers treating a patient. These professionals go beyond that with their kindness and treatment on a daily basis. I was so sick sometimes that just a smile and gentle voice made me feel things were going to get better. It is reality when I say the contact I had with each care giver did affect my outlook in a positive way.

We all know about the importance of healing from prayer through spirituality. I do not take lightly the love of my husband Willard and my daughters, family and friends as well as those around me praying for me. I am grateful for all that cared.

Writing gives me the opportunity to say thanks. And to present another type of healing that many have no awareness of. It is this healing that will be covered in detail within this book. It is healing from the visions I saw and the voices I heard. I received visions with messages that gave me great inner peace. These visions are hard to explain and mostly there is no way to examine them through scientific experiments.

I realize as I write I open the door for criticism from the doubters and disbeliever. I accept that; I do not have answers to the total phenomenon. I only know what I saw and heard was and will remain real to me. Writing about this phenomenon is difficult but it is my hope that explaining what happened to me will be viewed as another way to heal.

CHAPTER I
IT CAN HAPPEN TO ANYONE

It was February, 2008; the air was cold and crisp in Kennewick, Washington where I, Louise Ingraham, had now lived with my husband Willard for the last 30 years. This was home and I had always loved the quiet suburban neighborhood where we lived. Our home was comfortable and I enjoyed the tranquility of our backyard that Willard had carefully landscaped with trees and flowers reflecting each season's beauty. Our yard was and is a get away area from the summer heat with overhanging shade from trees and vines. During the colder season when plants and trees go dormant there is a feeling of freshness in the air that is invigorating.

As the days in that February month went by I, (Louise), was having my good days and bad days on how I was feeling. Except for a cholesterol problem I had no recent previous illness. Pain had crept upon me over several months beginning with discomfort and a dull aching pain in the lower part of my back to excruciating back pain. Not wanting to alarm my family I passed it off as old age creeping in; after all I was now 77 years old and after that many years of living the aches and pains were bound to appear. I had not expected though that after getting off my feet

FROM A PATIENT'S VIEW POINT

to rest the pain did not go away and was definitely getting worse.

We had lost our beloved pet Indy, a Maltese, in January and although she was 14 years old x 7 in doggie years and considered having a full life we had lost a great friend and mourned her passing. I even thought perhaps the stress of loosing her had brought on the health issues with my back. The only other complication I had was a higher than normal cholesterol count that I had under control with a statin drug.

One day rolled into another; on some days it was difficult to walk and almost impossible to walk up and down our stairs from the main floor to our entertainment and TV room. Thank goodness for the handrails; I did not want to give in to having Willard help me; at least not just yet.

It was March 2nd when everything came to a climax. I was in pain and agreed with Willard that we would get an appointment with our family doctor, Dr. Matt Smith, the next day. That night I watched TV sitting in an overstuffed chair with Willard sitting in a chair near me; during the evening I slept on and off sitting up while he watched TV. Willard helped me to bed at 10:00 P.M.

CHAPTER I: IT CAN HAPPEN TO ANYONE

I am hazy as to what took place next and am referring to the journals Willard wrote daily to tell the story. Willard speaks from this point on in his own words.

We retired normally at 11:30 P.M but this time it would be different as Louise wanted me to help her to bed at 10:00 p.m. Before putting her to bed I took her to the bathroom. When she was finished and ready to go to bed it was at this point that everything would begin to change for us over the next year of our lives.

It was a short walk to the bed from the bathroom but Louise could not stand up by herself. I am reasonably strong in my arms and thought it would be no problem to lift her up and help her walk to the bed but try as hard as I could using all my strength it became an impossible task for me.

I called my daughter Mary Ann and son-in-law Joe in Arizona. I remembered Joe had been a medic in the service so I was hoping with that experience he would know of a way to help me so I could get Louise into bed.

Joe's first question to me was, "do you have a big long bath towel handy"? I immediately answered that there was a bath towel hanging here on the towel rack. Joe proceeded to tell me to put Louise's arms around my neck and wrap the towel around her and under her arms using it to lift her up. I did lift her up then slowly shuffled with her toward the bed.

FROM A PATIENT'S VIEW POINT

As we got to the bed I wanted to gently help her down on the bed but instead she insisted she wanted to lay down on the bed on her other side. As I tried to maneuver her to her other side she collapsed slowly to the floor. I tried my best to hold her up but I couldn't manage to hold her from collapsing onto the floor

I immediately saw that I was not going to be able to help her up from the floor and get her into bed on my own so I called 911 for help; it was only minutes and the ambulance arrived. There were three attendants and they easily lifted Louise back into bed. I tucked the covers around her thinking sleep was what she needed most. She settled into a regular sleep pattern. It seemed the best plan was to wait until morning and then get her to our doctor.

It was the next morning on March 3, at about 7:30 AM that I placed my hand on Louise's forehead and found she was burning up with a fever. I borrowed a thermometer from our neighbors, Dilara and Jack Sabin, across the street so I could check Louise's temperature; I found it to be 103 degrees. Immediately I phoned 911 for an ambulance to take her to Kennewick General Hospital; they arrived in minutes. The attendants loaded her on a gurney and proceeded out the door to the ambulance. It was cold, very cold in the 30s that morning; Louise was awake enough to feel the cold through her pajamas and the light sheet the attendants had placed over her. I asked

CHAPTER I: IT CAN HAPPEN TO ANYONE

for blankets to cover her but because of her high temperature the ambulance attendants told me it was better to keep Louise cool and it would help bring her temperature down.

It was a short ride; about two miles to Kennewick General Hospital, photo below, where the ambulance

attendants admitted Louise in the emergency area for treatment. Hospital staff immediately took charge and proceeded with many tests and exams to determine the cause of the pain as well as the best way to bring down the high temperature. Dr. Matt Smith, our family doctor was called in. I was kept informed of the test results and was told Louise had a sciatic nerve problem plus a kidney function problem brought on by the sciatic nerve problem.

They connected Louise's kidneys with a catheter to drain the urine. The urine was quite red and sloughing off particles. It was also found that she had a lot of inflammation throughout her body. At the same time they were giving her intravenous fluids flowing through her kidneys to flush out the inflammation and to bring her temperature back down to normal.

The next day Dr. Matt Smith ordered an MRI to check Louise's problem further. It resulted in finding a growth was attached to the lower back sciatic disc. Dr. Smith also had a brain scan done to determine if the infection and fever had caused any brain damage. The brain test revealed no damage.

I credit Dr. Smith with his quick action in finding the cause then committing Louise to a specialist for further treatment. He made arrangements and informed me he was sending Louise by ambulance to Kadlec Hospital in Richland where Dr. T. Thomas Wilkinson, specialist would be in charge.

CHAPTER I: IT CAN HAPPEN TO ANYONE

It was 5 PM, March 4, 2008 that Louise was taken to

Kadlec Hospital in Richland by ambulance. She was placed in room 2035 and immediately there was a flow of doctors and nurses drawing blood and making various tests followed up with a decision that the next step was an operation was necessary.

There was a room full of nurses around Louise during prep time. Due to the infection in Louise's system her room was quarantined. Everyone in the room had to put on a yellow covering over their clothes that covered all the body. All the nurses hovering over Louise with me sitting back looking on made it appear like a bunch of yellow bees with their yellow shawls all hovering over a bee hive.

FROM A PATIENT'S VIEW POINT

Left photo is Dr. T. Thomas Wilkinson, MD Neuro Surgery, PS spinal and cranial specialist. He was the surgeon in charge and came in to talk to Louise and myself to tell us everything that was going to be done in the operation. At 9:30 PM Louise was wheeled from her room to surgery.

I waited in Louise's room and about 11:10 P.M Louise was brought back to her room. She was already awake and talking. Dr. Wilkinson went over with me what had been done in surgery. He had removed a growth on the lower disc of the sciatic disc area and cleared all the pus around the disc in the spinal cord area. The sciatic nerve was being pinched by the growth. He also readjusted the disc and cleaned it thoroughly. A short distance in the large back muscle he found the sciatic nerve being pinched by muscle and full of pus all around it. He told me the operation went well and he was confident that he had gotten it cleaned up and now was putting Louise on the road to recovery. He also said that if the

CHAPTER I: IT CAN HAPPEN TO ANYONE

problem had not been located soon the infection and growth would have damaged the lower sciatic disc to the point Louise would have lost the use of both of her legs. I felt fortune that Dr. Wilkinson was the one that had performed the surgery on Louise. He is highly regarded as a specialist and justifiably so.

I was told that somewhere in the beginning of Louise's problems she had contacted a staff infection that triggered all the sequences and more problems. The staff infection was not the worst infectious kind MRSA, but it was dangerous and had triggered the growth in the weakest part of the body as well as filling her body with infection and inflammation causing still more problems including improper functioning of her kidneys.

I tried to think of where Louise could have picked up the infection and thought of the prior visits we had taken to see patients in other hospitals. I was told everyone always thinks hospitals but the infectious virus could have been picked up anywhere from something Louise touched; even have been gotten from the grocery store where many hands have touched a grocery cart or almost anywhere.

I stayed all night with Louise that night. Nurses for various reasons were coming in and out of the room all night. Louise was full of tubes and she was on oxygen. There were many tests and medications through the next days. The nurses were wonderful

FROM A PATIENT'S VIEW POINT

and when Louise complained she was cold they brought pre-warmed blankets to cover her. There were tests and more tests also there were blood samples taken and medication given. Her vitals were good enough that I was able to go home at night but returned early everyday to spend the day at her bedside. She was having her troubles recuperating and on the 7th of March they rechecked her liver for possible damage.

Louise was very weak and unable to turn over in bed without help but always there were nurses with helping hands to make her comfortable. Our nieces, Janis McDonald and Loretta Rowlette with granddaughter Montana came to visit. The quarantine had been lifted and they were able to come in for a short visit. I tried to take photos of everyone but timing and access got in the way of photo opts and I was unable to capture everyone on film.
Verdell and Norman Ingraham, photo below of

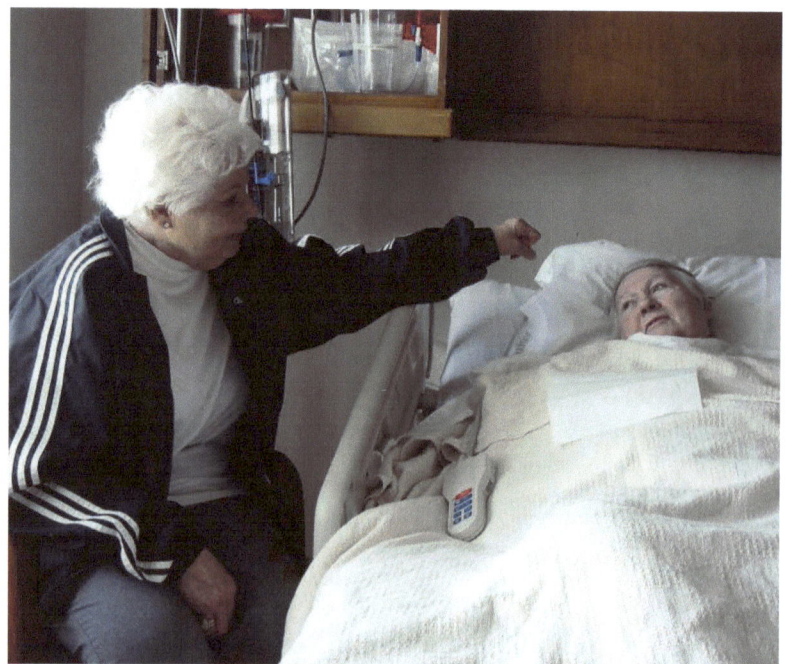

CHAPTER I: IT CAN HAPPEN TO ANYONE

Verdell, stopped by to see Louise. I was happy to see all of them; they brought smiles to Louise's face; their entire visits were uplifting for her. Verdell returned on other days as Louise was recuperating; she realized Louise's legs did not have adequate circulation and brought lotion and massaged her legs. The nurses kept vibration socks on her feet and legs at night but it was the massages that Verdell did that gave Louise the most comfort.

On the 8th of March the oxygen was removed but it still was difficult to get Louise to eat anything. She was weak and complained of a pain in her lower frontal area. Her system was full of infection.

The nurses were taking regular blood samples and sending them down to the lab for testing. Louise's arms were totally covered with black and blue markings due to numerous needle insertions to draw blood.

On the morning of March 9, 2008 as I was sitting in Louise's room when they sent a phlebotomist in to draw some blood from Louise's arm. The nurse tried for quite a length of time and finally gave up. They sent another trained phlebotomist in to see if she would have better luck, she did not have any better luck to find the vein in Louise's arm so they sent the third phlebotomist in to try her luck on finding a vein for a blood sample. By this time Louise's arm was turning blue from all the new punctures.

FROM A PATIENT'S VIEW POINT

When this nurse picked up a needle to draw blood I immediately exclaimed, "That is enough; there must be another way you can draw some blood." The nurse that came in looked up at me and quickly said, "yes, and I am going to do just that right now."

In about fifteen minutes Dr. Shirata came to Louise's room and installed a blood apparatus in the central blood line in her shoulder area. He installed three valves at this time. The nurses could now draw blood by inserting an intravenous needle. The nurses drew always four vials of blood each time. These vials of blood amounted to a lot of blood taken each time which prompted a question from me, "Why do you have to draw so much blood each time?" The nurse quickly answered, "because, the lab needs that much to do their tests."

Also on the 9th of March the nurses were getting Louise to sit up in a chair for therapy. I was encouraged but also knew she was so weak she couldn't sit long and still complained of pain in the lower part of the abdomen. I realized they were taking blood sample after blood sample for good reason. It was on the 13th of March at 3:45 PM they gave Louise a blood transfusion – 2 units of blood.

It was on the 14th of March they x-rayed her back and chest. The therapists came to her bedside and gave her breathing exercises as well as arm exercises.

CHAPTER I: IT CAN HAPPEN TO ANYONE

This morning they put a quarantine sign on her room for caution. All had to wear a shawl, mask and rubber gloves because she had contracted a light form of pneumonia.

On March 14, 2008 as I joined Louise in the morning we talked about her night and of coarse I got a full report on how she was progressing on her way to getting well.

She was not eating very much and had eaten very little from the time she entered the hospital because food did not taste good to her. She said when she ate her stomach hurt. This was a tremendous concern of mine because with very little food going into her stomach and taking large doses of pills each day it had to be irritating her stomach.

I asked the hospital to give me a list of the names of each pill administered to her and what was the reason for each pill. The hospital graciously presented me a list and I sent the list to our daughter, Mary Ann who lives in Mesa, Arizona. She went on line to the Mayo Clinic and researched the medicines Louise was receiving for side effects.

I remained at Louise's bedside everyday to give my assistance wherever I could by fluffing her pillow, giving her water etc. I stayed eight to ten hours a day.

FROM A PATIENT'S VIEW POINT

Each day I spent writing daily notes of her stay in the hospital.

The longer I watched the doctors and nurses caring for their patients and making them comfortable I have more respect for all of them dedicated to their jobs and doing so with a smile. I know how important it was to Louise and all the patients in hospitals.

Today Louise told me she had a vision the night before telling her that she would not get well until the doctors cured the hurt in her stomach. In her vision she had a view inside her stomach. Where there was a big glob of red bad stuff that must be gotten rid of before she would get well. She said she had a lump in her stomach that she could feel.

I immediately informed the doctors and nurses of Louise's vision telling them I don't know if any of you believe in visions but I know Louise and if she has a vision I would pay attention to it.

The nurses did pay attention and soon they had Louise examined then an x-ray tech soon brought an x-ray machine next to her bed and took several pictures to see if they could locate what was going on in her stomach.

The x-rays showed nothing that they could detect so the final diagnoses was it must be the pills that were irritating her stomach.

CHAPTER I: IT CAN HAPPEN TO ANYONE

During these last few days Louise had many visitors. Family and friends stopped by with best wishes, cards and gifts in hand (photo at left). One of the nurses called Louise's room Grand Central Station. The nurses too enjoyed the many flowers she received and would occasionally take a closer view of the display admiring the way the flowers brightened up the room. Dilara and Jack Sabin came by as did nieces Janette Burgess and Linda Giles and Dorothy Wolters. An old school friend, Clarence Wandling came by to say hello as did cousins Phyllis and Ray Dodson. There were cards, flowers and gifts sent by family and friends that lived out of town and had no way to make a one on one visit. Sister Nora Nelson from Salem, Oregon sent flowers and daughter and son-in-law Mary Ann and Joe Hicks also sent flowers.

Louise's most frequent visitor was Verdell Ingraham. She seemed to sense the need for more therapy for Louise's legs. The hospital staff was putting some kind of vibration socks on Louise's legs for circulation benefit at night. Verdell brought some lotion and very meticulously applied it to Louise's legs with a massaging motion. Those treatments were

FROM A PATIENT'S VIEW POINT

so beneficial to warm up her legs and gave her comfort from pain long after the massage.

During these days there were bedside nurses and caregivers coming in and out of Louise's room. There were a number of professional leaders and team members stopping by to examine Louise's medical charts and discuss their own findings with us. There was even a social worker stopping by to make sure we understood all the Medicare and secondary insurance procedures. Dr. Chow discussed with us the in patient rehab procedure.

Louise's bladder, kidneys and liver were trying to shut down and she still had infection throughout her body. The doctors and nurses were doing all they could to overcome all the problems and bring her body functions back to normal.

Dr. Obioma Onuorah M.D. Nephrology was a bladder

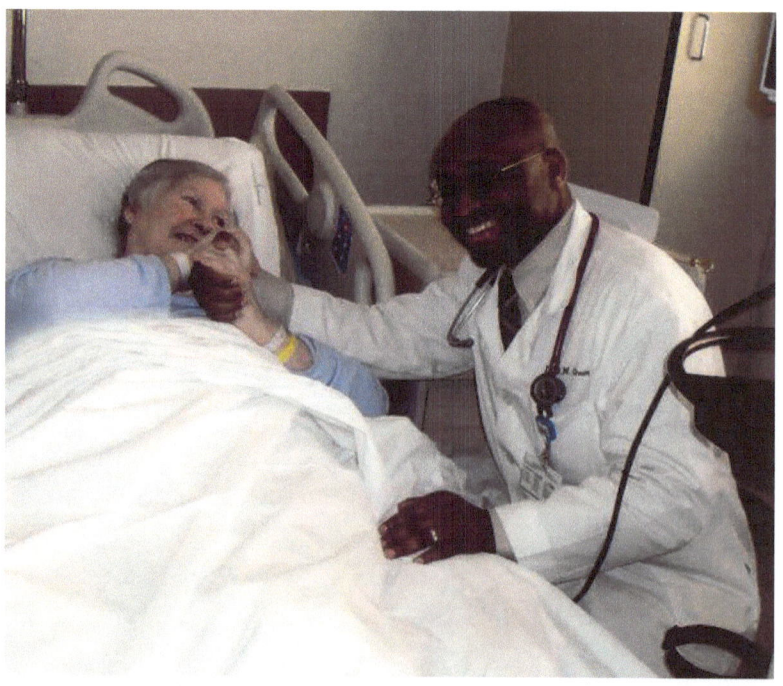

CHAPTER I: IT CAN HAPPEN TO ANYONE

and kidney specialist and viewed the lab findings', explaining what was happening as well as what to expect. Dr. Onuorah photo above during one of his patient visits. Louise seemed to have an immediate connection to this fine doctor and I was not surprised to hear him say, "I can feel your pain." Then Louise replied, "You are wise." There seemed to be a repertoire where his presence and philosophy gave positive thinking to Louise's mind that complete recovery was coming. Dr. Onuorah told her at one visit that he had talked to his sister in Florida and she too was praying for her.

It was on the 14th of March that Louise told me of yet another vision. She saw very clearly a blue sky and many people trying to help her. The picture of their faces floated in the sky seemed to her to be a good thing. She was seeing all the people that were helping her get well in the hospital. The warmth she was receiving from seeing them said that they cared for her and were giving their help freely for a recovery. She watched the vision intently with a warm feeling as the sky slowly turned to a pinkish blue and the faces floated away and the vision was gone.

Was this the medication talking; I don't know and neither does Louise. She says though that it does not matter where it came from; it was real in her mind and was helping her to move one step closer to complete recovery.

FROM A PATIENT'S VIEW POINT

Having visions and messages were not unusual for Louise. Under confinement in a hospital and the circumstances of her condition the visions were highly valued for the peace they brought with them.

During Louise's treatment I took photos of all the hospital staff and care givers that I could with their permission to put them to print, although, unfortunately there are many missing that came to her room when I wasn't there or their services were outside her room, yet, indirectly related to her care. I was grateful to have the opportunity to record each day in a journal along with photos that show how caring each person was in Louise's time of need. I feel they are on the front line in a patient's overall needs and do not get enough recognition.

I now present many of these professionals.

FAREED ARIF, MD
NEPHROLOGY/
HYPERTENSION
SPECIALIST

CHAPTER I: IT CAN HAPPEN TO ANYONE

Louise tells me that she does not like the many photos of her but I have convinced her that giving justice to those who cared for her were photos taken at her bedside and each in their own way speak volumes in their concerns for their patient. As you can see from the photo below Louise was in need of various equipment and medical aid to sustain her and professionals to monitor them. She was recuperating from back surgery, had infection through her body and pneumonia crept in to add to her problems.

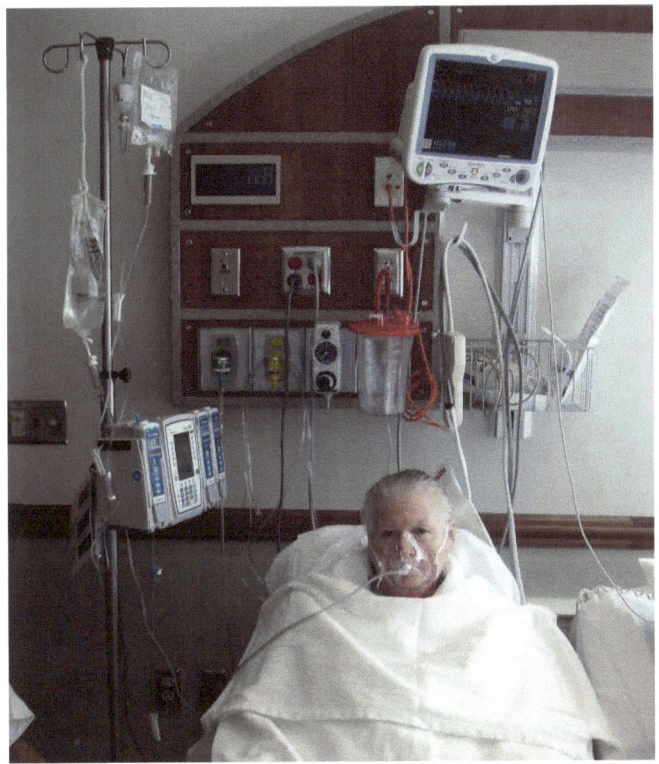

FROM A PATIENT'S VIEW POINT

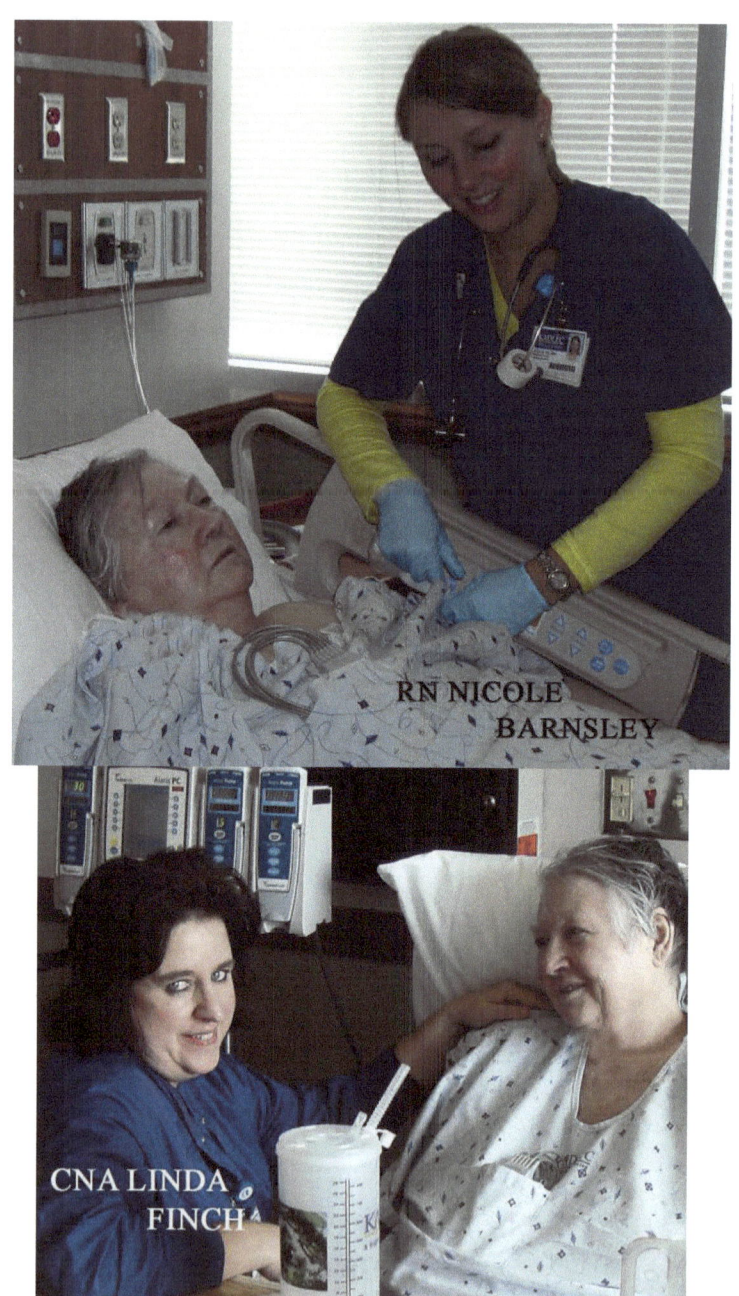

CHAPTER I: IT CAN HAPPEN TO ANYONE

Each professional had a medical purpose to see Louise but they all brought encouragement in how they handled their tasks at hand.

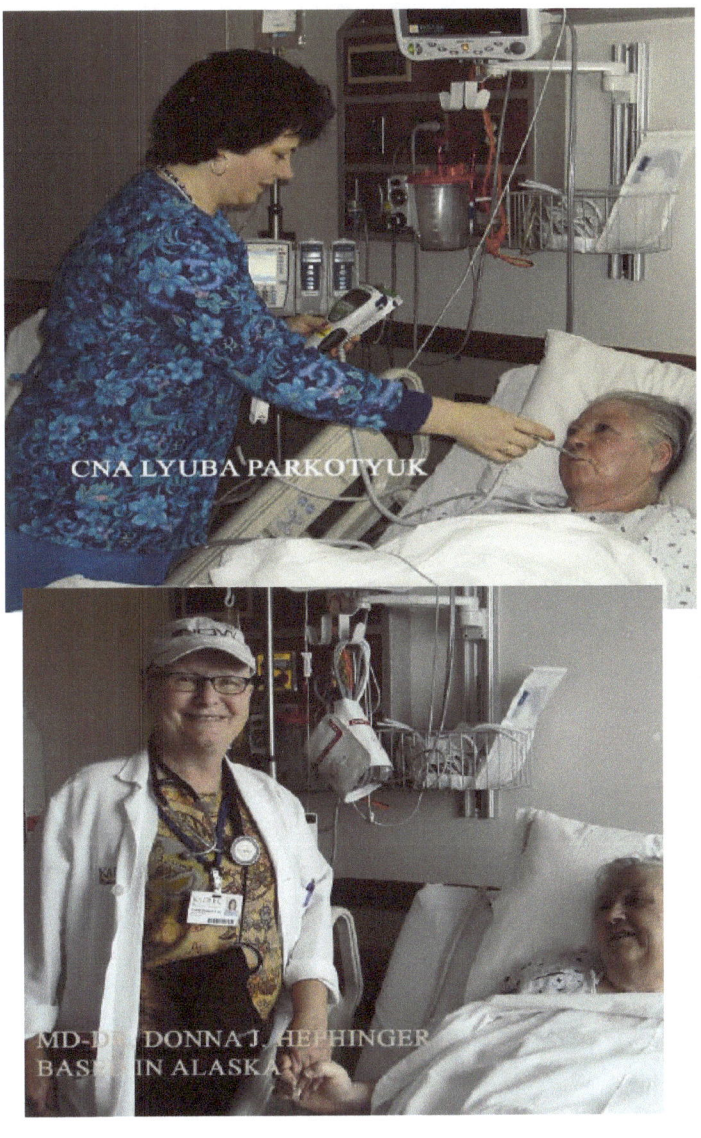

FROM A PATIENT'S VIEW POINT

Dr. Hephinger, MD came to monitor care.
Jennifer came with a smile to check Louise.

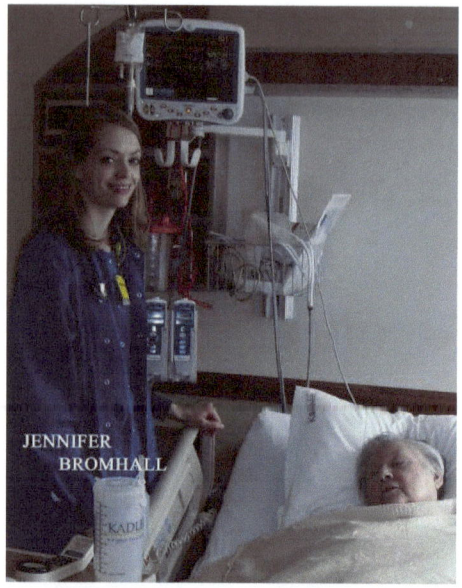

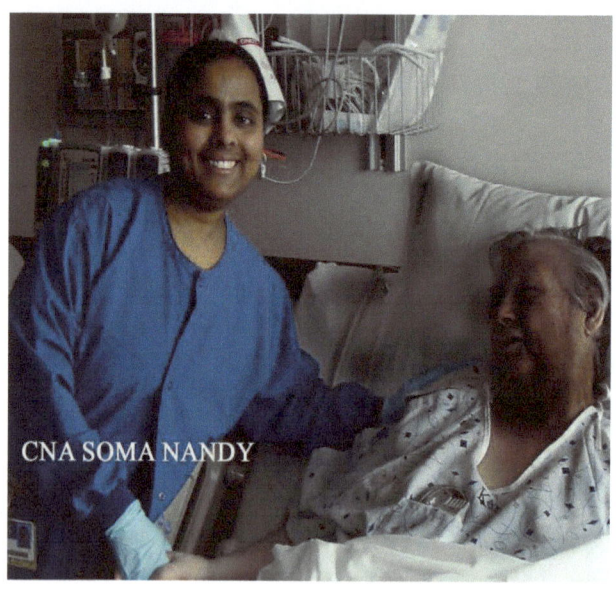

CHAPTER I: IT CAN HAPPEN TO ANYONE

Soma Nandy had to wear gloves as required but was giving her patient heads up with a smile.
Louise is now sitting up even though a long way from being well.

RN Chante Madison and RN Karen Madeson knew from talking to Louise that she loved having young people around and brought in Kayla Madeson (9yrs old) for a short stay. The visit cheered Louise up.

Therapists tell us that young visitors make older people smile but I can tell you first hand that with Louise it was the youthful exuberance Kayla brought that was uplifting to her mind.
It was like a breath of fresh air brought into a sick room that was infectious.

FROM A PATIENT'S VIEW POINT

The days past and I could see the positive results of all the care but Louise wasn't eating and complained of pain in her stomach. RN Brenda comforted her.

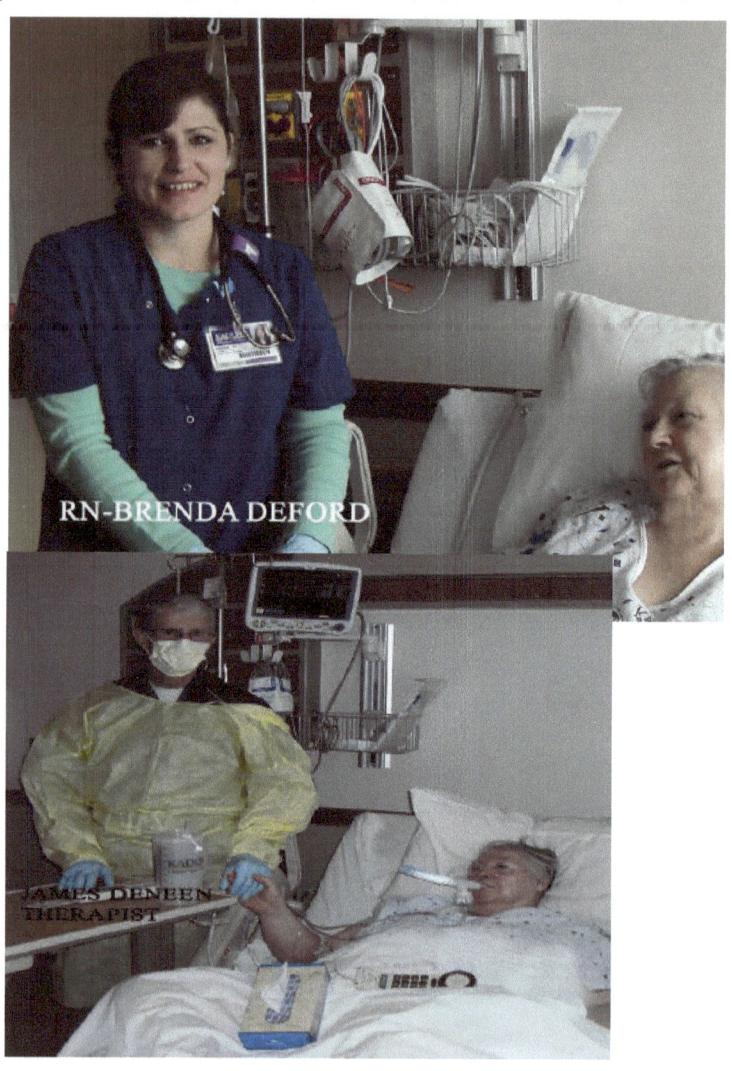

CHAPTER I: IT CAN HAPPEN TO ANYONE

James Deneen, therapist came wearing a yellow cape. Louise is taking a call on one of her better days.

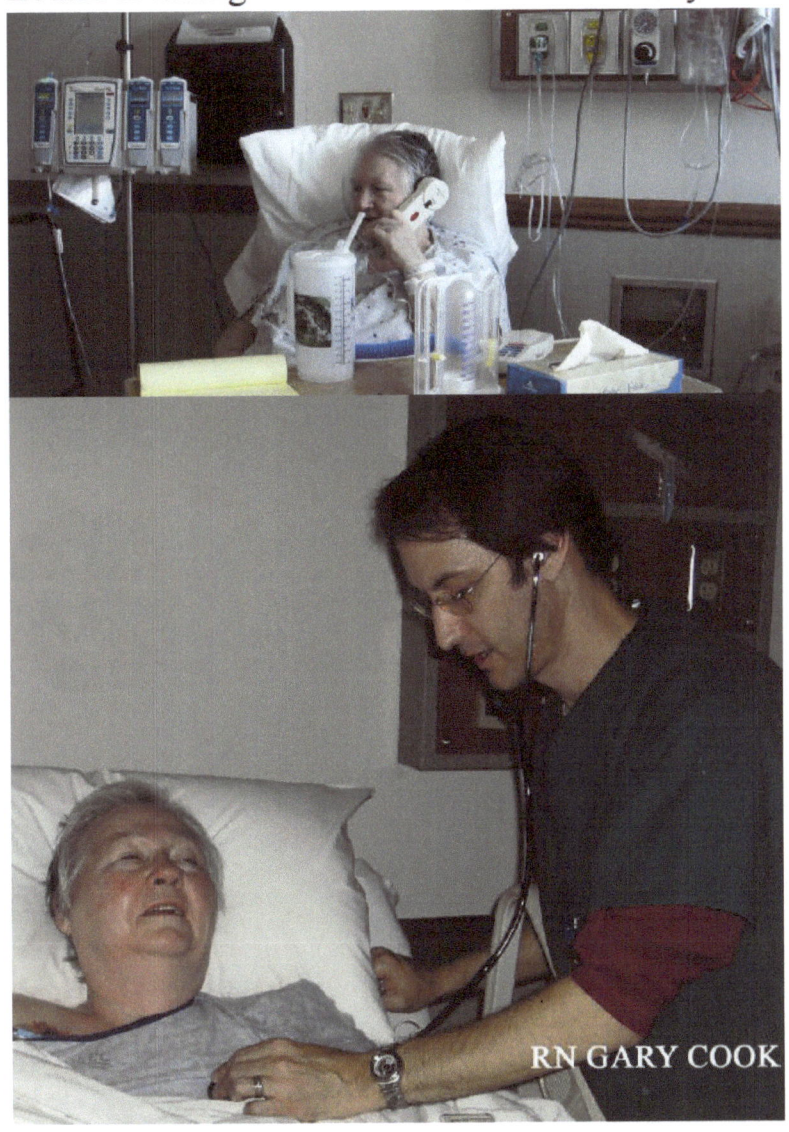

During the recuperating stages at a hospital the charts are monitored on a continual basis and as soon as it is

feasible the patient is put into therapy. Louise still had the pain in her stomach; she complained also of a bad taste in her mouth. She was able to sit up in bed and they proceeded to schedule her for therapy.
The first step is to get the patient to sit up in a chair which they did for Louise with helping hands.

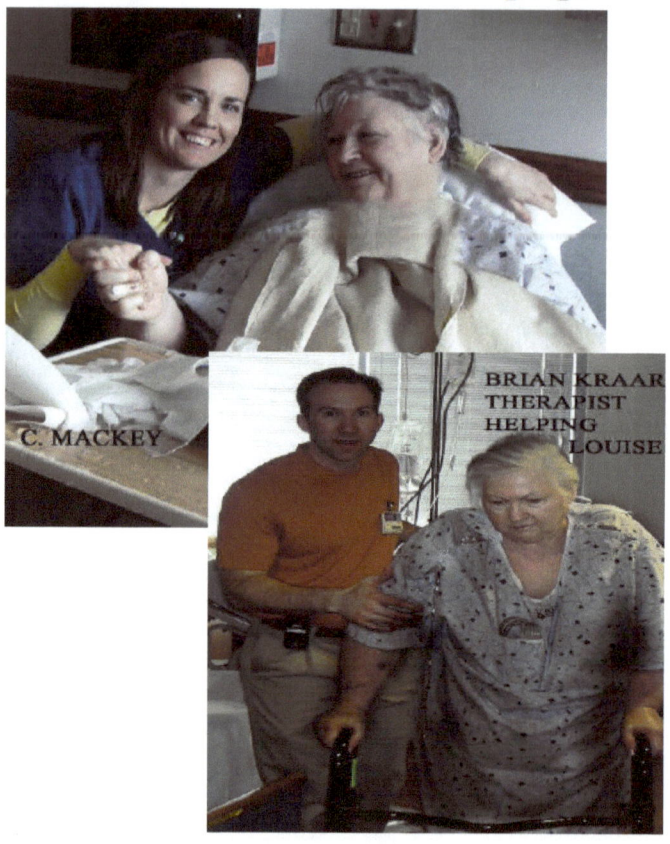

Brian Kraar, therapist got Louise up into a walker.

CHAPTER I: IT CAN HAPPEN TO ANYONE

There was therapy done also while Louise was in bed.

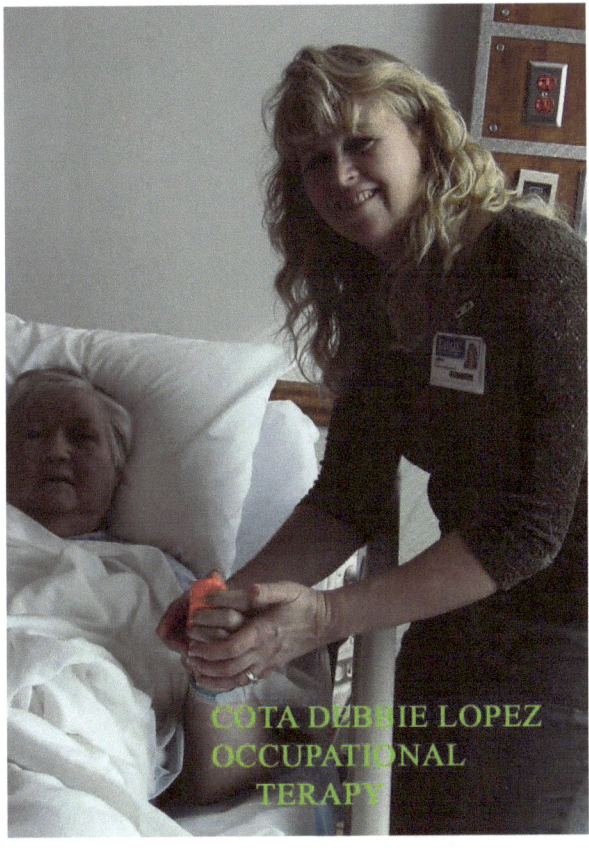

Debbie was helping Louise with hand therapy.

Through all of this in the beginning, after surgery, Louise could not turn over in bed by herself nor help herself with any of her needs. There were always professionals to help her through these trying times. No wonder she saw all their faces in a vision one night as those who gave her care and kindness.

FROM A PATIENT'S VIEW POINT

Linda Jensen, NRT came in with paper work.

Even with wonderful care there were dark days ahead for Louise.

CHAPTER II
TIME STOOD STILL

I believe it is timely for me to explain more specifically how Louise's visions came to be a part of her story when she was in the hospital. Everything has a beginning and my awareness of her insight was disclosed to me before we were married. Louise told me this phenomenon has been a part of her life as far back as she can remember.

Louise and I have been married 62 years last September and during that time I have been confronted with a power she seems to possess that brings messages and visions to play out in her mind as if a video is playing in colored photos with voice. I have never doubted that what she sees and hears is real. I understand that to clarify the process I need to start with her beginning. I must also make a personal statement of the reality of what she sees. I pay attention because her visions always bring a powerful message that adds truth and meaning to our life and others.

Louise explains that receiving the visions and messages are gifts that are allowed to be received from a higher power that she refers to as God. She says it is important to know you may call the higher power any name but to Louise the name refers to God. She also receives messages through entities called souls. These souls (entities) live in living forms of energy throughout space. They have passed on from life as human souls on earth at death to live on; they never die as the body dies at death.

I will stop right here to further explain that Louise believes a soul leaves the human earthly body at death and lives on forever in the form of energies. The soul takes with it not only the energy of the soul but the mind of the person it is leaving to continue living together into another time. Within these energy forces that soul has the power to connect and communicate with the living on earth. She calls this soul an entity that she communicates with through using thoughts. She tells me one only has to believe it is possible to communicate.

You might ask why not only God? I realize it is complicated but the difference between communicating with God is God's messages can come with asking or come without asking while a message from an entity is communicated only after asking a question using our thought process.

She has explained to me that all these messages are received by hearing a voice or voices through her thought process. She says it is as if she has a direct electrical line open at all times that is connected as one energy force to another. It is like a positive and negative battery creating energy that communication takes place through. Our souls and minds are made up of energy forces as are the entity (souls) made up of

CHAPTER II: **TIME STOOD STILL**

energy forces. She refers to the entity messengers as her spiritual connections through the use of energy forces and electromagnetism.

The communication, she declares, are from souls (entities) that have passed from life to live spiritually in another dimension. She sees them as total energy forces in many colors. It has been told to Louise that because the mind and soul are forever together their energies change in color with different experiences. In other words, different colors of each soul's energy represent the many experiences that a soul has had over time. It is simply an energy force that living souls (entities) can have a constant connection through.

Calling this communication a gift is explained by Louise as a gift allowed by God that everyone can have but not all are aware of. She emphasizes gifts can come in different manners but no ones gift is more special than any other person's gift.

Louise explains that each of us has a soul containing an energy force connected to the mind in the brain that holds all past and future memories that can be called upon as we wish. In the beginning of all life this higher power determined that the soul's energies would not survive without growth of the soul. Sharing by communication allows the spiritual side of the soul to grow.

FROM A PATIENT'S VIEW POINT

Louise readily admits there is no scientific proof of what she has found from her own communication. She only knows the energy flow between souls is always present. If you believe you too can tap into it. Realizing there are contradictions and ridiculing when soul communication through thought process is brought up she chose for years not to discuss it openly. As she has grown older she is now convinced it is her due to reveal what she has experienced to help others open the same doors of communication should they desire. It remains a personal choice to believe or not to believe and everyone's right to do so.

I listened as she explained that her gift first appeared to her when she was a little girl and she saw happenings before they occurred. She refers to one most vivid memory of seeing the family pet ran over with a car and it was found later to have occurred. When Louise was younger speaking out about her revelation brought on ridicule from others. She was told she had only imagined seeing a vision before it happened and was confusing reality with the way she wanted to believe. In her child like mind she determined the best approach was never to tell anyone what she was seeing for fear of being called a liar.

Louise kept this pack with herself until just before we were married and then she revealed to me what she was seeing and hearing on certain occasions. It was proof to me that there were insights here although I

CHAPTER II: TIME STOOD STILL

could not understand at first the huge impact it would have on both our lives.

There is much more that can be said on this subject but the forgoing explanation will allow the reader to have a sampling of Louise's views as I disclose to you what happened during her hospital stay.

It was after the surgery to remove a growth on Louise's back that the first hospital visions appeared. She was being treated with antibiotics including other medical treatment for complications. Her system was still full of infection. Vivid visions were appearing. I will describe to you what Louise saw and heard while lying in her hospital bed.

The room was quiet and she was wide awake. She was on oxygen and did have medication being administered regularly. Nurses were going in and out of her room. Louise had contracted pneumonia and because of the infection in her body there were a few days that quarantine was again placed on her room. The yellow capes came out; anyone entering her room had to wear them including myself. Louise called them, "the yellow birds." Staff was attending to the tubes connected to her, administering oxygen and medications as well as taking blood samples; all for around the clock care.

Louise repeated to me in great detail what she saw vividly reflected on the hospital room wall over the foot of her bed. She said it was night time and the room was nearly dark except for dimmed light. She was wide awake but had her eyes closed when she heard the voice telling her you are seeing the "Purpose of Life". The following is what she told me the next day.

It was on the morning of March 15, 2008 when Louise described her vision to me. As she explained to me what she had seen it filled my mind with so many pictures. I said, "Let's go through the vision a step at a time while I write details down and maybe I will be able to capture every picture you saw on paper."

It took me several days to get all the information from Louise because all day long nurses and doctors were checking her periodically. Between her medical care, when we were alone I began to write down every step. It was a slow process but Louise assured me with each step that it was what she had seen in her vision.

She told me to picture a big square in the center of other squares surrounding it; all the squares had a pinkish cast, more like sepia color. In the center of the big square was a descending dove, thus symbolizing the Holy Spirit. All around the big square was smaller squares. The total vision covered the entire wall as she viewed it lying in her bed and seeing it on the wall from looking over the foot of the bed.

CHAPTER II: TIME STOOD STILL

Each square had a symbolic significance. I have numbered them left to right as she saw them pictured on the wall to explain what vision was in each of the squares and what they meant. Remember they are all in sepia color.

1. Jesus sitting on a rock; symbolizing Jesus watching over everyone for God
2. A barber's pole; signifying the growth and direction of life.
3. Picture the scene of a stream of water cascading down the mountain; signifies the flow of life.
4. Praying hands; signifies keeping prayer in your life.
5. Picture a little girl with Jesus' hand held over her head; signifies Jesus' power over every thing.
6. Picture the moon shining on the ocean; signifies and reflects the direction of life.
7. Picture the sun on the horizon; signifies expanding the mind.
8. Picture the sun set with a rainbow above the sunset; signifies reflection of life.
9. Picture using thought process from you to your entities' and out to others; signifies communications.
10. Picture a pyramid; signifies where the soul goes beyond.
11. Picture galaxies of stars in space; signifies the soul lives in the beyond.

FROM A PATIENT'S VIEW POINT

12. Picture a dark hole with icy surrounding; signifies you must not get lost in life.

PURPOSE OF LIFE			
#1 JESUS WATCHING OVER EVERY ONE FOR GOD	#2 BARBER POLE GROWTH AND DIRECTION OF LIFE	#3 STREAM OF WATER FLOW OF LIFE	#4 PRAYING HANDS KEEP PRAYER IN YOUR LIFE
#5 PRAYING HANDS OVER LITTLE GIRL JESUS POWER OVER EVERY THING	A DESCENDING DOVE THE HOLY SPIRIT		#6 MOON SHINING ON THE OCEAN DIRECTION OF LIFE
#7 SUN ON THE HORIZON EXPANDING THE MIND			#8 SUN ON HORIZON & rainbow REFLECTION OF LIFE
#9 ENTITIES THOUGHTS COMMUN-ICATION	#10 PYRAMID THE SOUL GOING BEYOND	#11 GALAXY & STARS SOULS LIVES BEYOND	#12 DARK HOLE IN SPACE DO NOT GET LOST IN LIFE

Louise and I have discussed her vision many times. I could not give you an exact copy of the pictures in her vision but above is an illustration of the layout.
She never questioned what brought the vision to her mind so vividly. She did ponder over each symbol and the significance of the purpose of life the symbols represented. She felt she saw them for a reason and there were directions and implications in each symbol for her awareness. It was all like a road map and her

CHAPTER II: TIME STOOD STILL

life was destined by what she had seen. I too agreed with her. What she had seen was uplifting to her.

I too, as does Louise, believe there is a cross over between medical science and our spiritual belief. Louise and I both know without a doubt if it were not for the hospital care she would not be here today. The science of it all prevails. We are fortunate to live in a time that so much specialized medicine and care is available. Having said that I believe it is in our future to have even more answers for preventive health issues and medical treatment along with understanding other means of healing as in the vision Louise saw.

I smile when I think of the many caring hands around the clock that were there for Louise's needs. The hospital staff recognized the benefit of the spiritual side and Louise was grateful as was I for the pastor's visit to her bedside with prayers and well wishes. At this time in Louise's recovery we knew from the pain she was having and the tests still revealing infection that she was a long way from being out of the woods so to speak.

FROM A PATIENT'S VIEW POINT

CHAPTER III
A STEP FORWARD IN RECOVERY

It was on the March 17, 2008 that Louise was moved to another area in the Kadlec hospital to room 421 on the fourth floor. Although she still had that persistent pain in the lower part of her abdomen I was elated to know they had removed the oxygen and the move was made to get her ready for rehab. My elation was short lived.

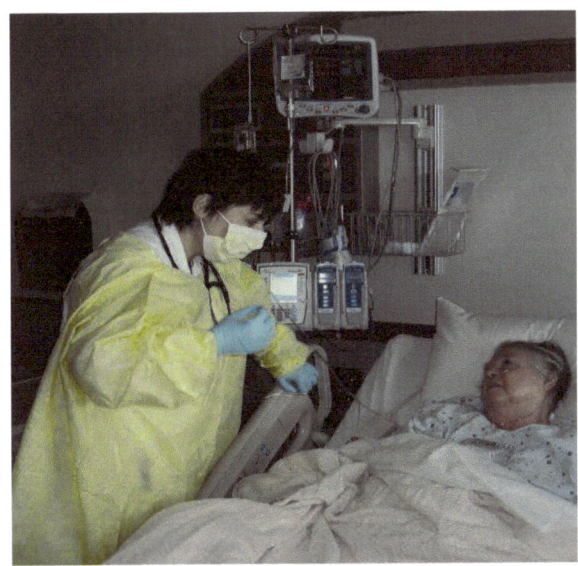

Dr. Olympia Tachopoulou, (photo below) a doctor of infectious diseases visited Louise. She was from Thesalonian in Greece and besides her professional view of charts and tests that were done she was very interesting. We had visited Greece a number of times and were interested in their culture and history; she talked of a Pinnacle Mt. near there and told us to check the internet for a full description.

FROM A PATIENT'S VIEW POINT

Dr. Tachopoulou had many concerns over the infection Louise still had in her system although the surgery done on her back was healing nicely.

We thought it was another red letter day when on March 18, 2008 they removed the catheter from Louise. She now could walk a few feet to the bathroom although she needed help.

We were also told that day that Louise would be moved to Kennewick Life Care Center in Kennewick, Washington for rehab. There was a rush to prepare her for the move. There were last minute checks and removal of all tubes and I-V from her.

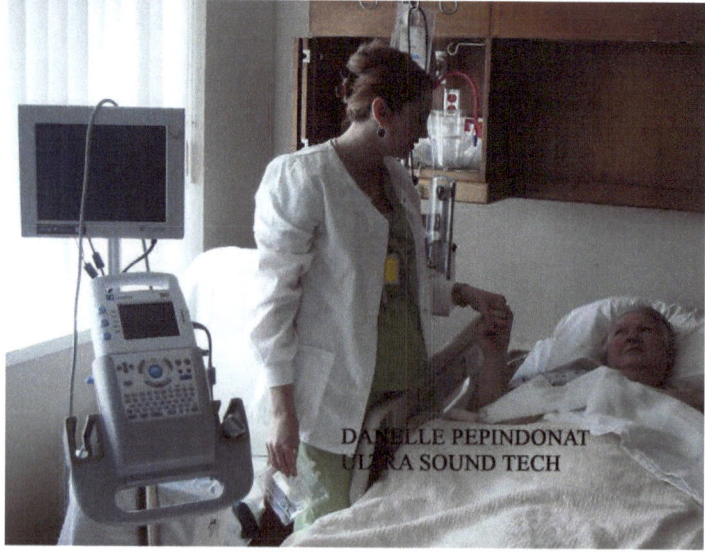

They brought RN Denell Pepindonat, ultra sound technician, in with the ultra sound machine to give Louise a thorough examination at her bedside. It was a lengthy test that took a great deal of time.

CHAPTER III: A STEP FORWARD IN RECOVERY

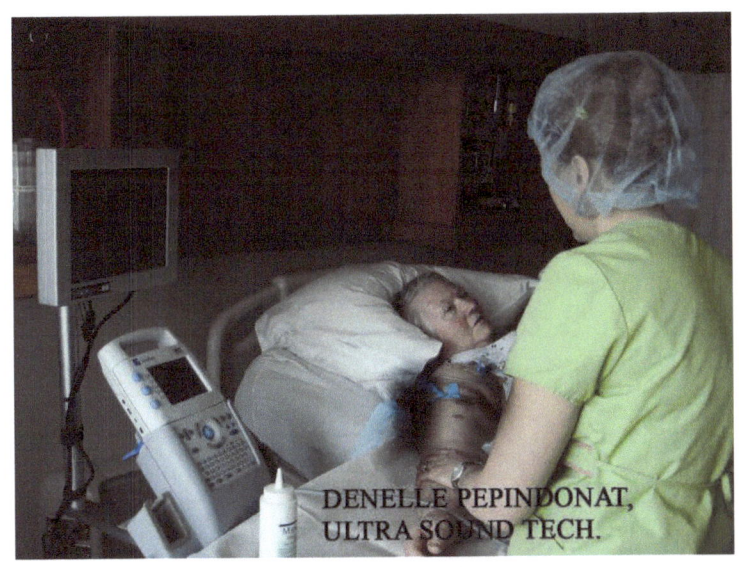

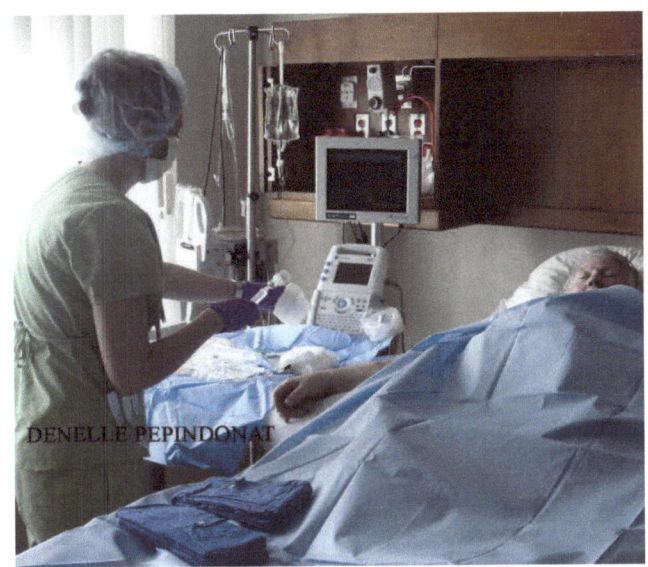

It was an interesting procedure to watch.

I took a number of photos of all the procedure.

FROM A PATIENT'S VIEW POINT

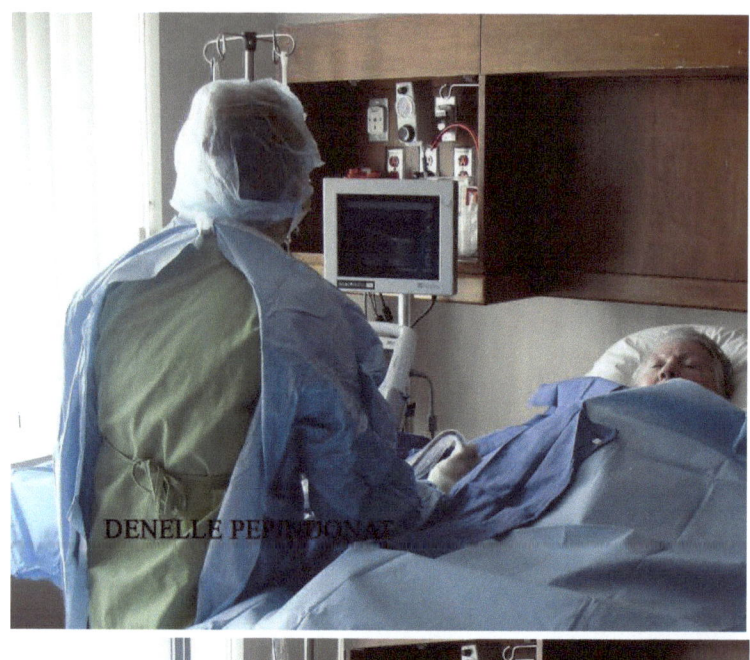

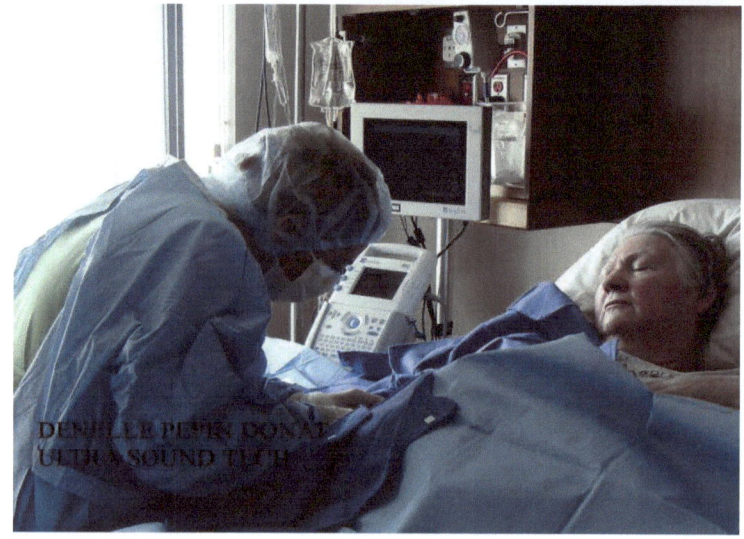

Louise was comfortable through it all.

CHAPTER III: A STEP FORWARD IN RECOVERY

I have two more photos of Denelle.

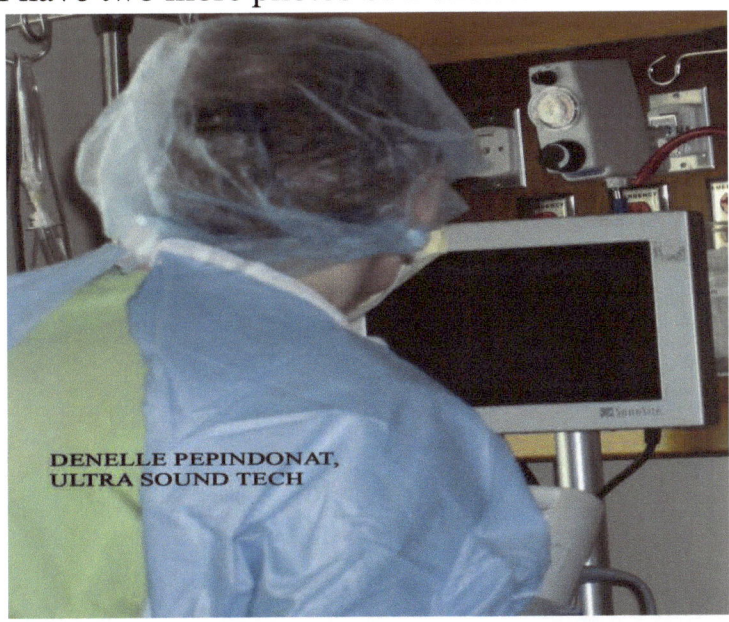

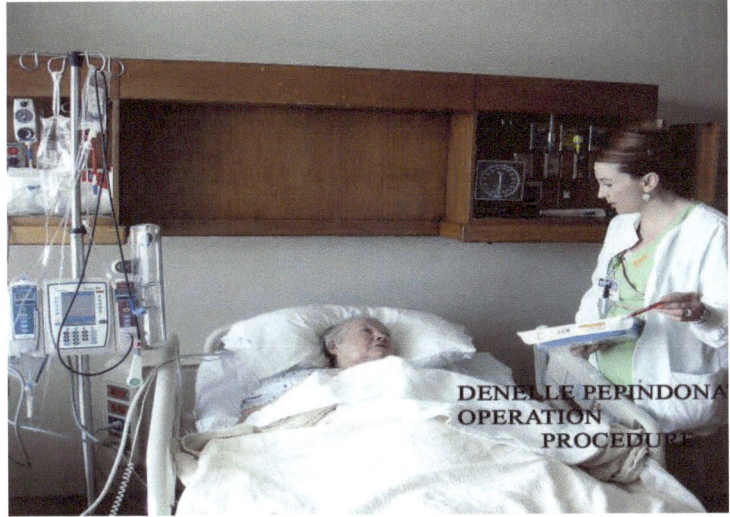

Denelle even took time to explain the results to Louise.

FROM A PATIENT'S VIEW POINT

Next Robbie Burch, X-ray technician brought in an x-ray machine next to Louise's bed and took several x-rays.

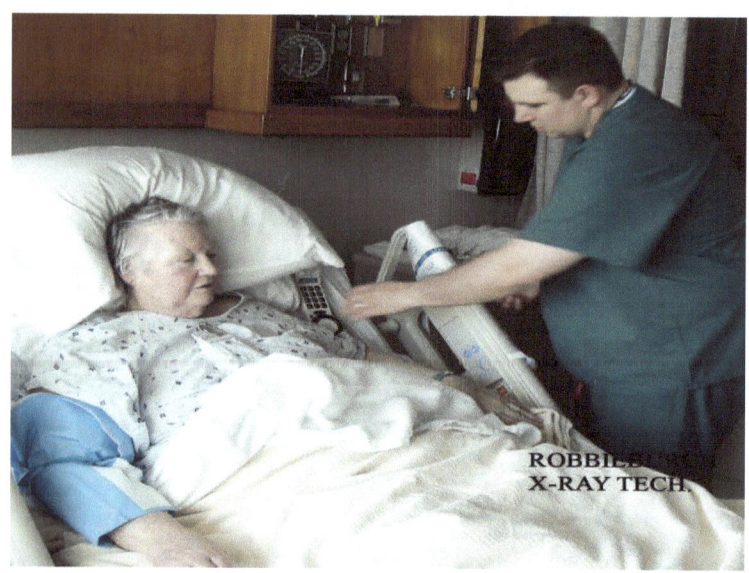

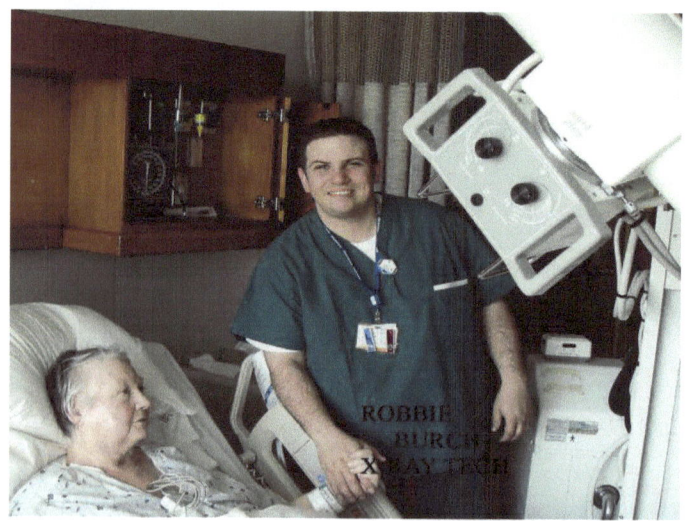

There was a complete medical check done in preparation for transfer.

CHAPTER III: A STEP FORWARD IN RECOVERY

C.A.N. Kevin Parker therapist came into her room and gave her therapy exercise.

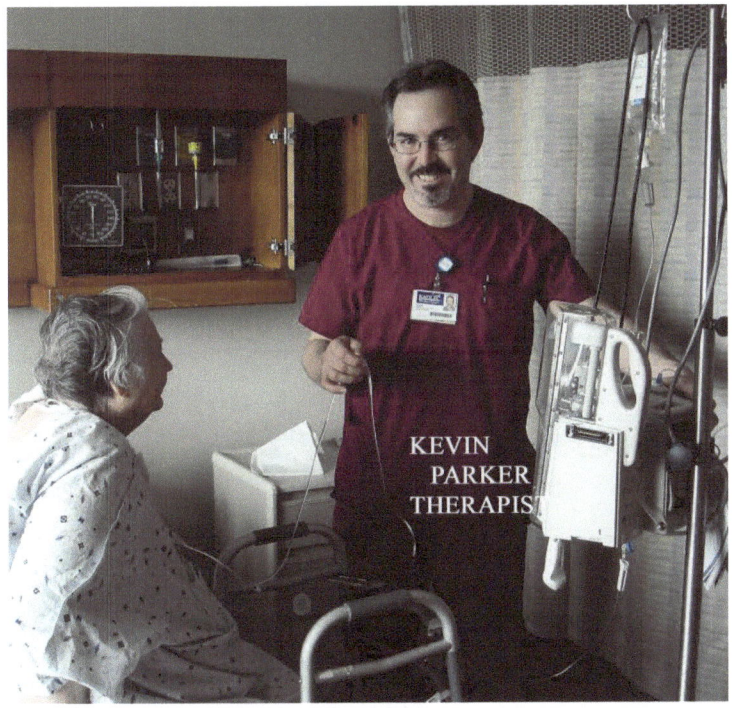

At this point of time there was a question if Louise would have rehab here at Kadlec Hospital or at Kennewick Life Care Center.

It was only after all the test results were seen that we were told Louise was to be released to the Kennewick Life Care Center. Louise was anxious to go as it meant two things to her; she was in a recuperating stage to have a release accepted and the care center she was going to would be closer to home for my visitations. She was still very weak and that persistent pain never went away.

FROM A PATIENT'S VIEW POINT

CAN Darcy Acevedo made a last visit to Louise's room before the ambulance arrived.

At 5:30 PM the Prosser Ambulance service from Prosser, Wa. came to pick Louise up and transfer her to Kennewick Life Care Center. I couldn't figure out why a Prosser service was coming into Richland when the transfer was to Kennewick but was told that the ambulance service that was available when a pickup was called in was how it was handled for efficiency.

CHAPTER III: A STEP FORWARD IN RECOVERY

The two ladies, Rebecca Shahaw and Brenda handled the transfer from Kadlec very efficiently.

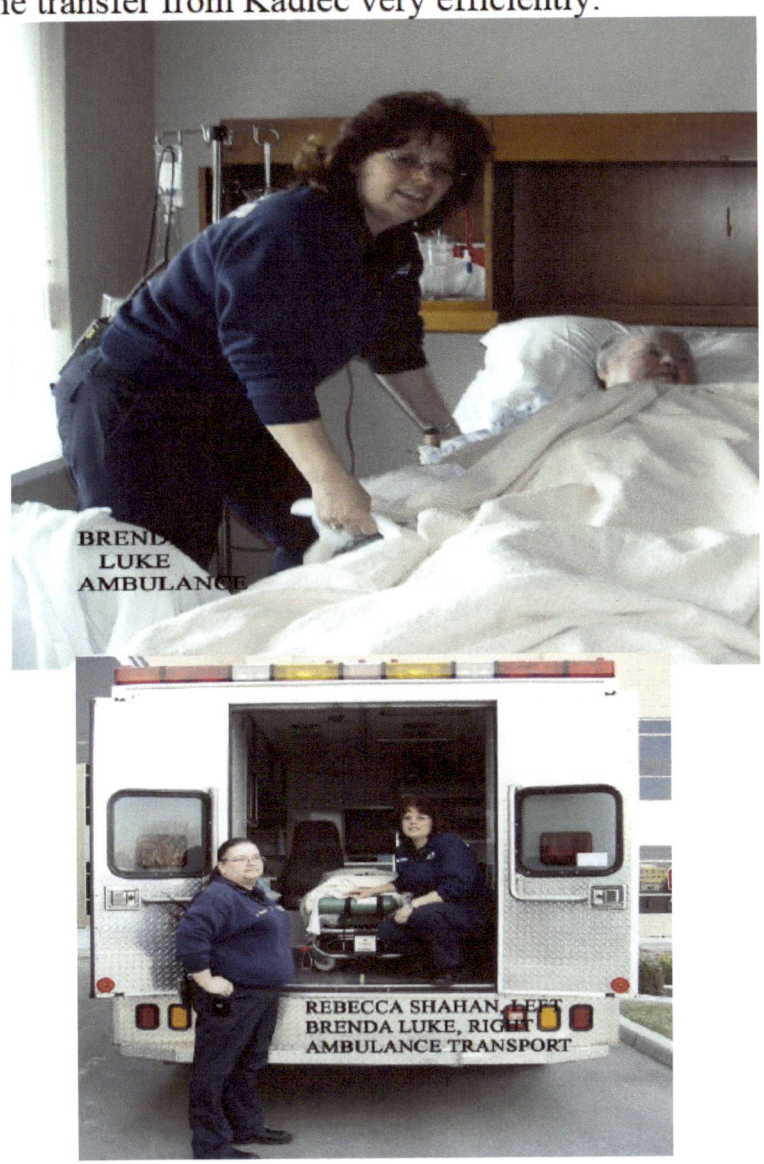

FROM A PATIENT'S VIEW POINT

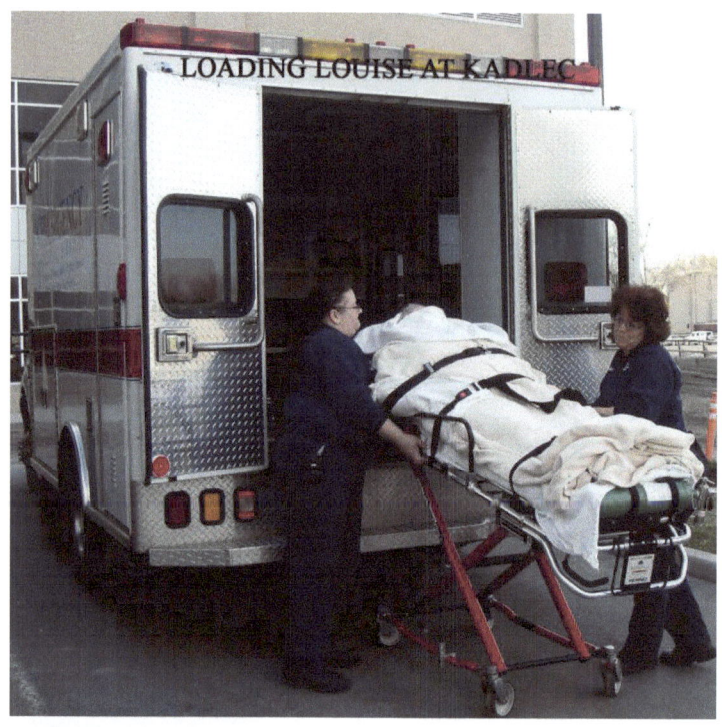

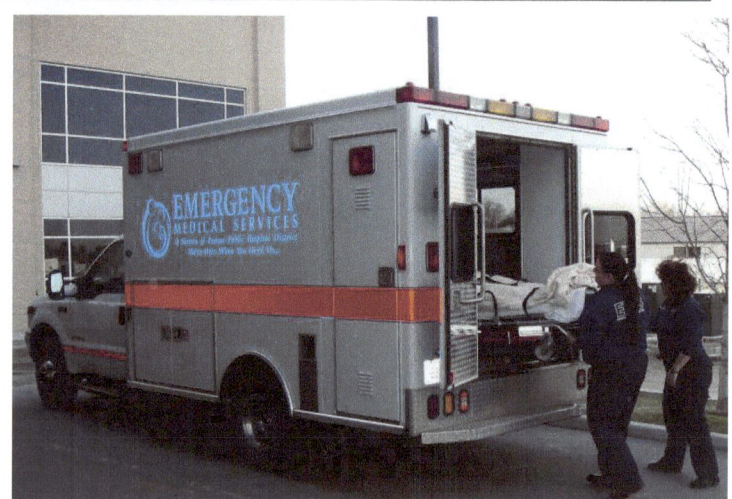

CHAPTER III: A STEP FORWARD IN RECOVERY

It was a short run from the Kadlec Hospital in Richland to the Kennewick Life Care Center. The Life Care Center of Kennewick is only a couple of miles from our home.

I was at the nursing home by the time they had Louise in her bed and settled into her room #320. When I entered her room I asked Louise if there was something I could get for her at this time and she said that she was bleeding and needed a nurse which I got for her immediately. The nurse said she needed help to roll Louise over onto her side to see her back and I volunteered. I had helped at Kadlec hospital at times to roll her over onto her side and knew what to do but the nurse said no that they had nurses here that can help. Before they rolled Louise over I asked them to be careful because she had just been operated on a few days ago on her back and had a long incision that was not yet healed.

I saw that when rolling her over a part of the incision was pulled loose on her back where the stitches were. The nurse quickly taped the incision and assured me that all was OK again.

There were further adjustments to be made for Louise's care as they still needed to catherize three times a day as her kidneys were not yet functioning right. She was extremely weak and the pain in her lower abdomen remained constant. They were medicating her yet for infection.

Of course the first thing on the list next to do was getting four vials of blood again for blood work. I explained to them the problem that occurred at Kadlec in finding veins and it was necessary to insert three valves in the main line artery in the shoulder to draw the required blood.

LPN Roger Potts and LPN Susan Gorbett were assigned to do the task. At first they wanted to try the veins in the arm but soon went for the valve insert in the main line artery in Louise's shoulder.

CHAPTER III: A STEP FORWARD IN RECOVERY

I knew this type of insertion was necessary but I could not help thinking why hadn't the valves been left in that was inserted at Kadlec.

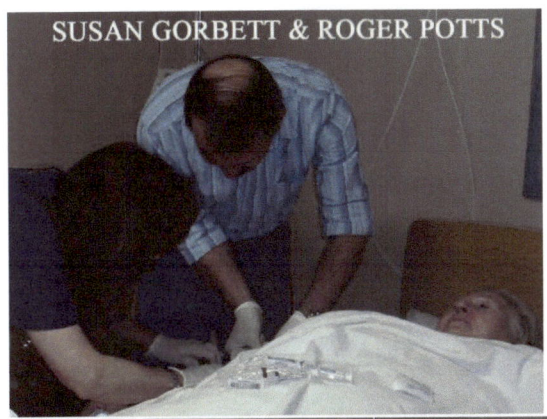

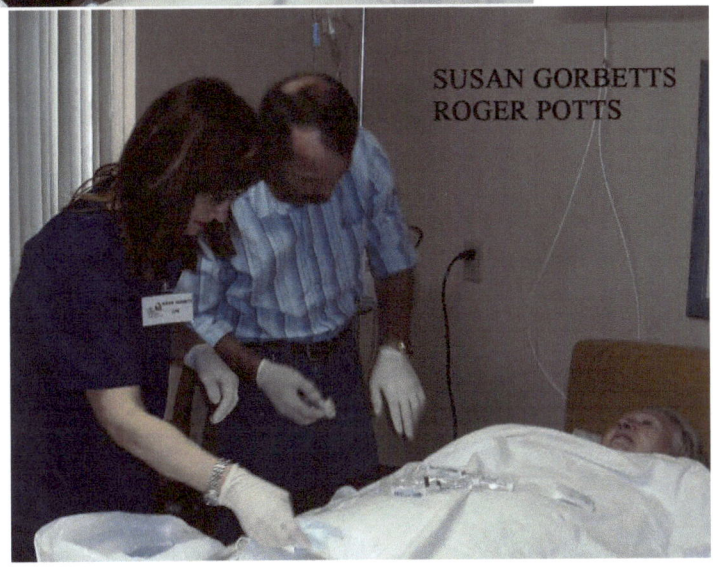

Roger Potts and Susan Gorbett worked together like team members and went from the arm veins to the shoulder to insert the tubes for drawing blood.

FROM A PATIENT'S VIEW POINT

When the job was done there were smiles all around with Jocie Gage joining in.

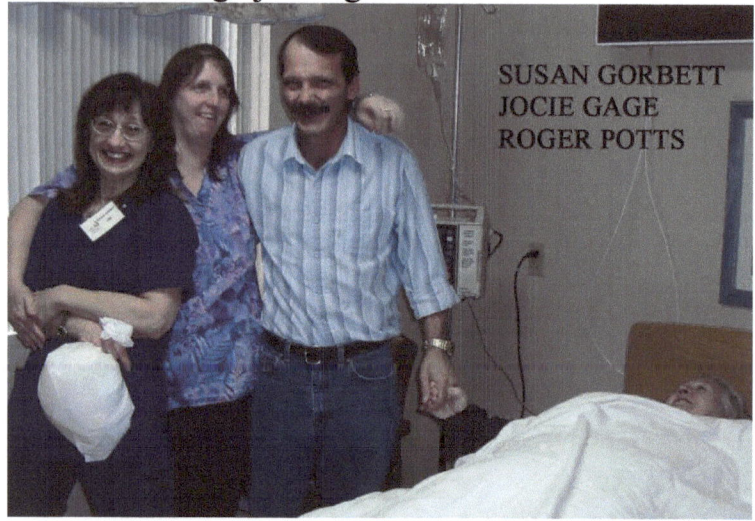

SUSAN GORBETT
JOCIE GAGE
ROGER POTTS

When family and friends found out Louise was in the nursing home they sent a lot of beautiful flowers and plants to our very special person.

CHAPTER III: A STEP FORWARD IN RECOVERY

Louise was an unhappy camper when the meals rolled around. Her stomach still hurt and food did not taste good to her.

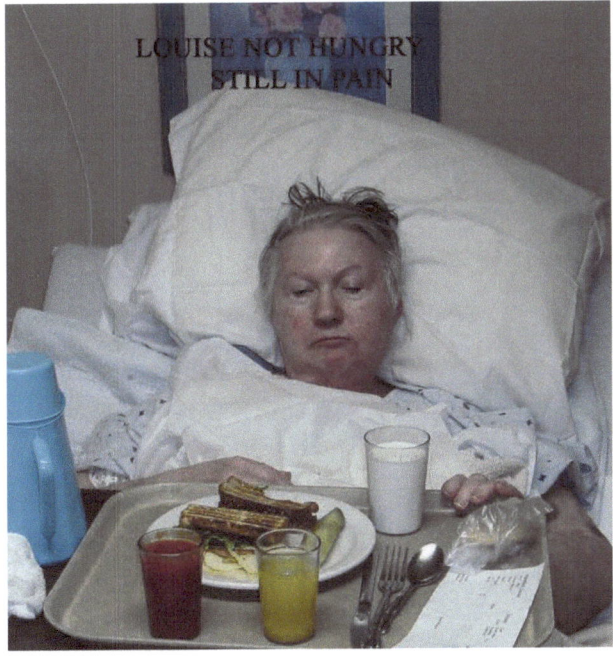

Louise had a nice room and the life care personnel were kind and efficient. I came everyday to stay with her as I had done at the hospital. After 3 or 4 days we had gotten acquainted with staff and one nurse noting I was there everyday brought in two cookies; one for Louise and one for me. Later another two nurses on seeing I was there everyday thought I should have a comfortable chair. Here they came with a very nice cushioned rocking chair with a matching rocking foot

FROM A PATIENT'S VIEW POINT

stool. It was an appreciated consideration beyond the call of their duty; their kindness is still remembered.

Lucy Soto and Elsa Salas saw to it that Louise got her meals and also the little extra comforts of the day.

Jane Robinson, receptionist always had a friendly greeting with a smile.

Linda Garwich had the hard job of shuffling the patients and other people at

CHAPTER III: A STEP FORWARD IN RECOVERY

Kennewick Life Care Center and to help the handicapped to where ever they needed to go.

Norman and Verdell Ingraham, Lorraine Johnston and many other friends and relatives came to see Louise. Their company and visits were uplifting to her.

Jenny Schwaab, dietary mgr. came to talk to Louise to see if she could fix something that she would like. Jenny wanted to entice her into eating again.

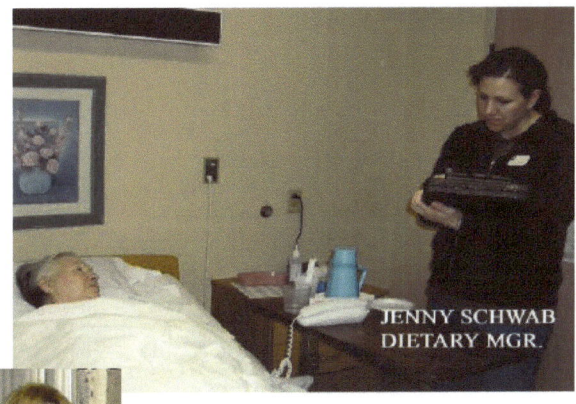

Everyone was so caring; Carolyn Conley, social worker graciously with another nurse brought a comfortable rocking chair to Louise's room for me to use; another big thank you Carolyn. I don't have a photo of the other nurse that helped with the chair.

Unfortunately I could not take photos of all the staff that was deserving of credit for their round the clock care. I was not there for the night or early morning

FROM A PATIENT'S VIEW POINT

shifts. Also I could only take and print those photos of persons with their approval. If there are any errors in names and or titles I assure you it was accidental.

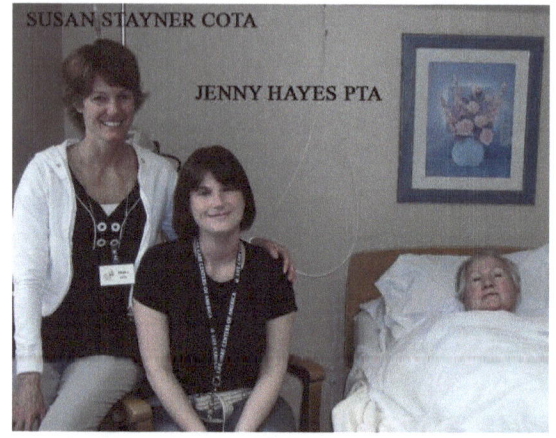

Susan Stayner, Cota and Jenny Hayes, PTA tried so hard to get Louise to do exercises. It was to no avail because she did not feel up to the task at that time.

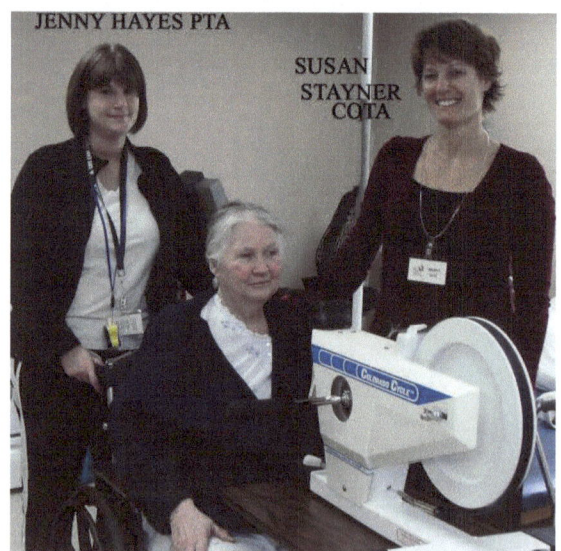

It was not until later and Louise had another set back did we realize why any kind of exercise was difficult.

CHAPTER III: A STEP FORWARD IN RECOVERY

Pam Haven, LPN, Elizabeth Murocna, and Hannah Goetz, CAN were always there to make Louise comfortable.

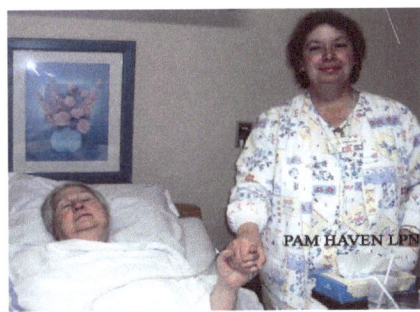

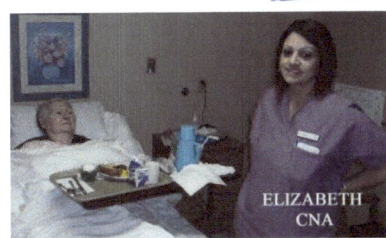

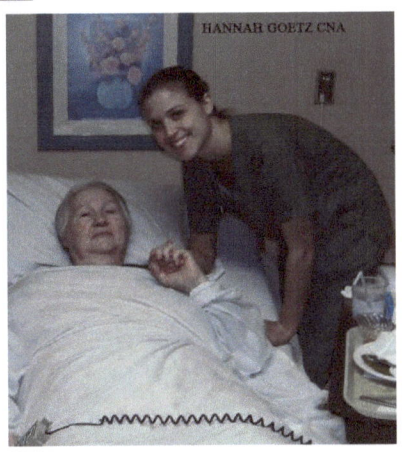

FROM A PATIENT'S VIEW POINT

As you can see Louise was treated royally by all the staff as were the other patients.

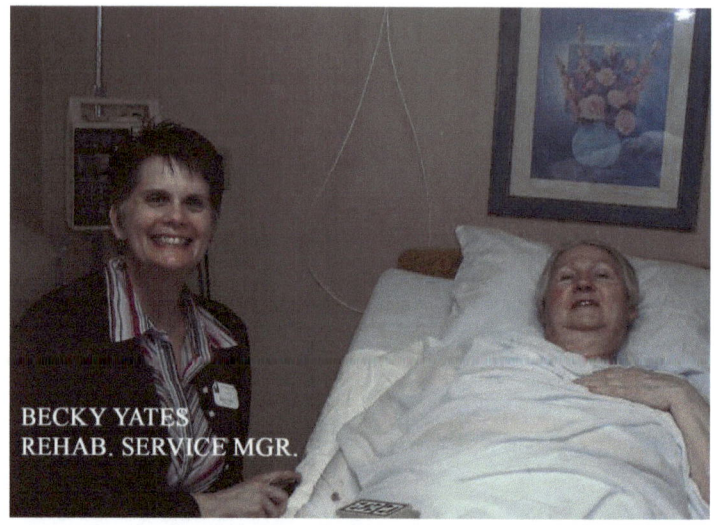

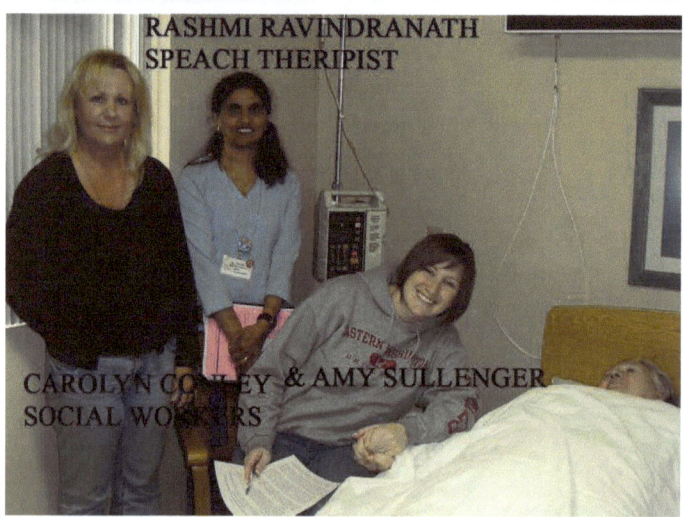

The staff asked Louise if she would like to join the others in the dining area but she declined. The idea of

CHAPTER III: A STEP FORWARD IN RECOVERY

eating was not on her list of musts except for the fact she wanted to recover and needed strength.
Trina Daves, RN, BS Director of Nursing periodically visited Louise's to check on her.

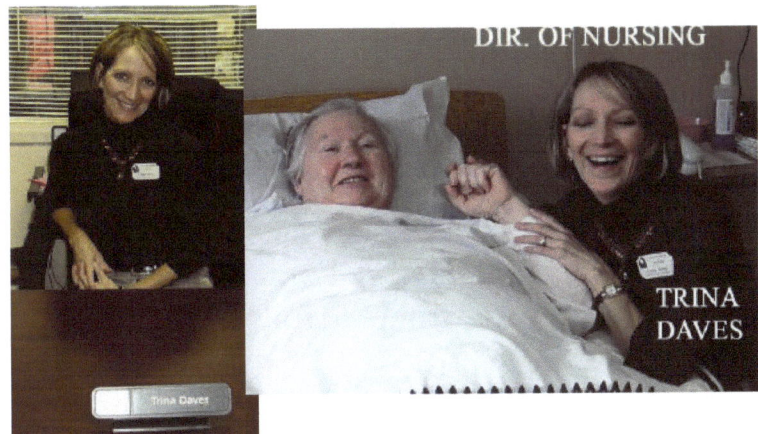

They have a great activity director, Brigit Jhanson; she planned activities all could enjoy.

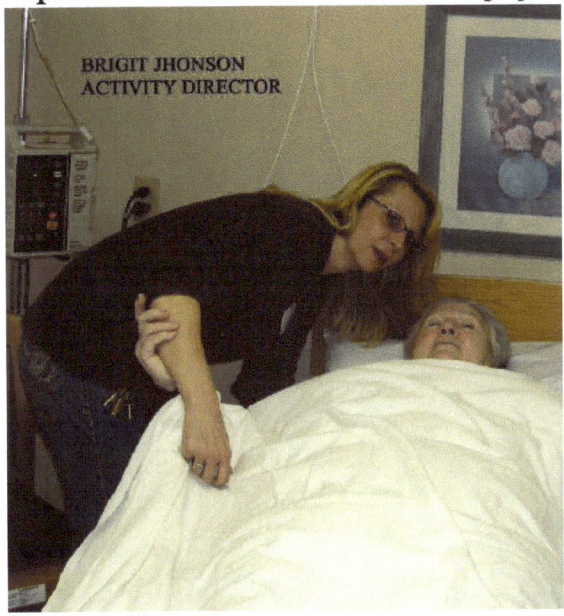

FROM A PATIENT'S VIEW POINT

She came in to tell Louise of an activity.

It was the 22nd and the Lifecare center was having an Easter egg hunt outdoors on the front lawn with a bunny bringing goodies for the children of the staff and families. Louise wanted to watch the fun and when it was found the wheel chair she would be using hurt the surgical area on her back a nurse came with a more comfortable wheel chair. The outing was brief but watching the children gave Louise genuine pleasure as you can see from the following photos.

TERESA CAPERON AS EASTER BUNNY

Teresa Caperon was the Easter Bunny for the Easter egg hunt. I took pictures and later when ask by a staff member if they could have copies I had a set made and gave them to the staff to enjoy.

It was cold that day and everyone bundled up to keep warm. Many of the patients were in wheel chairs. Watching the children of the employees and

CHAPTER III: A STEP FORWARD IN RECOVERY

others brought smiles on the faces of those watching the fun.
Louise was given extra blankets to cover her head from the cold that day.

The Easter Bunny was the highlight of the children. It looked as if some of the patients were sleeping but for the most part even those who had difficulty sitting up

FROM A PATIENT'S VIEW POINT

straight were doing their best to taken in as much as they could of the action around them.

More Easter photos:

CHAPTER III: A STEP FORWARD IN RECOVERY

It was a day Louise still talks about. When it is said, "having the young around brings joy to all and has a special meaning for those in a care center" she agrees. I went home that evening as I did every evening. I was thinking things are looking up for Louise's full recovery; what I did not know was that just around the corner was yet another enormous trial for Louise to endure.

FROM A PATIENT'S VIEW POINT

CHAPTER IV:
   MIXING SCIENCE WITH SPIRITUALITY

It was on March 26th at 5:20 A.M when a nurse at the Lifecare Center called me (Willard) to inform me Louise was bleeding from the mouth and nose. She was also vomiting up blood and they had called an ambulance to take her to Kennewick General Hospital.

I arrived at Kennewick General Hospital (photo above) before the ambulance and had to wait before a nurse came to the front desk so I could sign Louise into the hospital. I asked the nurse if she would please call me to the room they had for Louise as soon as the ambulance arrived. She said she would do that.

When the ambulance arrived with Louise blood was still coming from the corner of her mouth. They unloaded her at the emergency entrance at the back of the hospital and wheeled her into emergency care.

FROM A PATIENT'S VIEW POINT

Louise was calling for me and I immediately joined her and held her hand as a bunch of nurses and doctors were hovering around her like bees around a honey comb.

They had placed her in ICU (intensive care unit) and pumped the blood from her stomach stabilizing her. Then they gave her 3 units of blood. I asked them if I should move so they would have more room to work; they told me to stay right where I was and they would work around me. Louise was aware that I was there and clutched my hand and would not let loose.

After they pumped the blood from her stomach they installed the necessary tubes and had her stabilized with monitors in place. They administered three units of blood intravenously. The color returned to her face indicating she was feeling much better. Most of the nurses had left her by this time except for some specialist to continue monitoring the situation.

Dr. Matt Smith, our family doctor was still there. I asked him if he knew what the problem was. His response was that he was quite sure it was bleeding ulcers but said more tests would be taken.

By this time they were ready to take Louise from ICU. She was watched continually and other tests were to be given to her the next day.

CHAPTER IV: MIXING SCIENCE WITH SPIRITUALITY

I went home that night like I had every night from the beginning of Louise's ordeal after eight or ten hours at the hospital. Normally I got home by 8:00 PM each night. I would take care of our little Maltese pet dog and make myself an evening meal, read the mail then spent an hour on the phone answering many calls.

Our daughter, Mary Ann Hicks, who lives at Mesa, Az. from the first day Louise went into the hospital was going to get on an airplane and fly up to help me. I insisted that Louise was now in the hospital where she was getting all the expert help she needed so there was no need to come home as everything was under control. It was hard to keep her from coming and only under one condition would she agree to do so.

Mary Ann told me she would agree if I would promise her that I would call her every night regardless of what time I got home. I told her I did not like to do that because some nights might be late and I did not want to wake her up. She told me if I did not call that she would be calling me so I agreed.

When I called her I would always say this is my bed check call then follow with a report on Louise's progress for the day. I felt now that Louise had to be brought back to the hospital again the root of some of her problem would now be located.

I had two big concerns along the way about Louise's stay at the hospital. One was she had no appetite and

FROM A PATIENT'S VIEW POINT

would only eat very little. The second concern with her not eating and getting something in her stomach was that she was given multiple pills that were bound to be irritating her stomach.

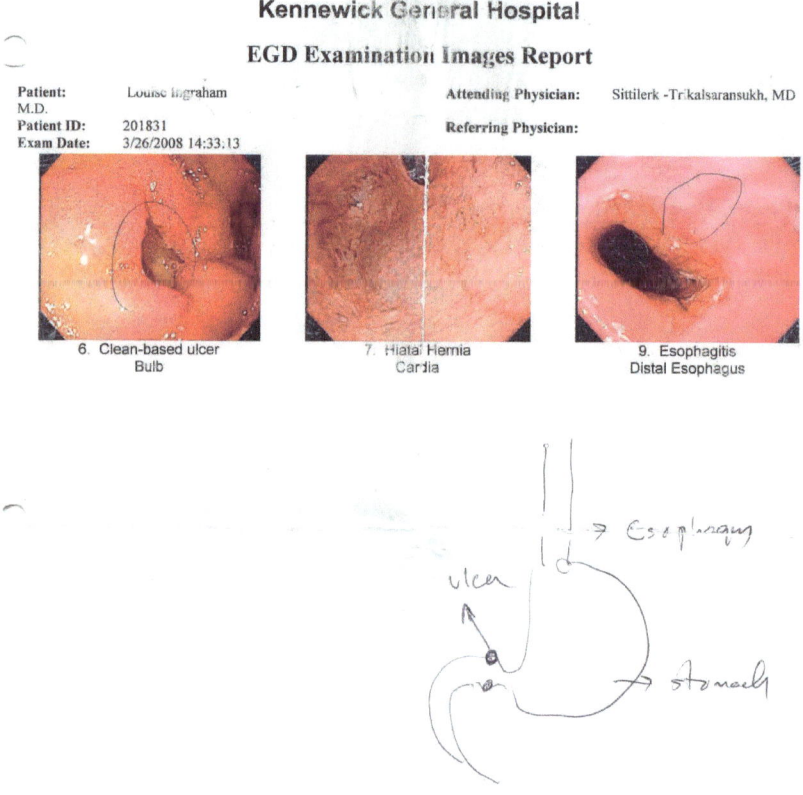

Back at the hospital Dr. Sittilerk-Trikalsaransukh MD came to Louise's room bringing in a lot of technical equipment. He did an endoscopy down her throat into the stomach with a lighted probe to get a picture to see what was going on in her stomach, (photo above).

CHAPTER IV: MIXING SCIENCE WITH SPIRITUALITY

The result was a clear colored picture of two big ulcers that was causing her the pain she had been having. The Dr. gave me a copy of the pictures he took showing the ulcers (photo on preceding page). They looked exactly like the vision Louise had been telling me she had seen which I will cover later in this chapter.

The nurses had not allowed me to stay in the ICU and watch the endoscopy operation but politely asked me to go to the waiting room. In about a half an hour or more the doctor came to the waiting room and explained that the operation went very well. When the endoscopy was done they also had the means while looking for the problem to cauterize the ulcers at the same time thus searing the sores and beginning the healing process.

The doctor did some kind of laser treatment and said with medication in four or five weeks there would not be any sign of ulcers ever having been there. Louise's pain immediately disappeared after the procedure and she truly began feeling better.

Louise recalled asking for me at the Life Care center and that I was at her bedside at Kennewick General but did not remember much else except for another vision she had gotten during that time.

This vision was described to me as follows: Louise told me that during or after the procedure in the operating room, she was not sure of the time; she was confronted with a dark void full of energies that completely surrounded her. The darkness was filled with what she called electromagnetism representing the presence of living souls that had passed from earth.

She felt her own being was not a body as known on earth but a spiritual form of energy held together by energy forces in a cluster. Seeing beyond her own being she saw the same type of spiritual energies each in a cluster of energy forces representing many souls all around.

She said she knew what she was seeing was her but anyone viewing her would only see many colored energies swirling around in a close compact form.

The energies she was seeing in her mind reminding her of electrical charges in many colors clustered each in their own confined area. Each cluster of colored energy represented a soul and all were floating in a black dark void space that seemed to go on forever. Each cluster of colored energies represented a living soul. Each living soul of clustered energies represented one life and included within the soul was that soul's ability to know of its previous, present and future life. She knew it to be the mind of each soul as part of the whole soul.

CHAPTER IV: MIXING SCIENCE WITH SPIRITUALITY

There was no light or tunnel as so many describe a death experience. It was only darkness and masses of energy but oh so peaceful. She was not afraid and there was no pain as she waited for further instructions.

Then a deep voice said to her, "you are not going anywhere; you have books to write." Then there was no voice and silence; she says she can not remember anything more until later the doctor and nurses were speaking to her as she came out of the darkness.

Talking about this later to me was difficult for her; she said she felt like she was in a place where it was determined if she would stay on earth or go beyond. She did not want to go but her fate was decided by someone else and it was not frightening.

Louise has never called it a life or death experience because she did not know if she was or wasn't close to death at that time. She did know that they had pumped her stomach of blood from bleeding ulcers and she was on oxygen at the time. She was given blood transfusions and she was in an emergency care status. I never thought she was going to leave me but it was critical to my thinking.

Again I questioned Louise about her vision and she replied, "I know it is difficult to understand and to even believe but it did happen. It is vivid and I was ready for whatever faced me. They weren't ready for

FROM A PATIENT'S VIEW POINT

me to go on and sent me back telling me I have work to do yet. I realize it was a critical time but I shall never fear when the end does come. For now I am grateful and will recuperate as I do have work to do."

For two days they kept Louise at Kennewick General. She again had visitors that lifted her spirits. I went down stairs in the hospital to the café for a sandwich while nurses were caring for Louise. I met Angel Trump who worked at the hospital and at one time had been an employee where Louise worked at the bank.

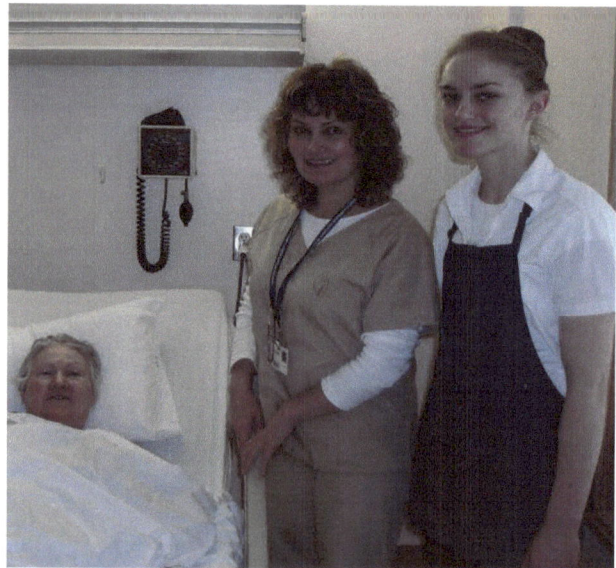

Angel recognized me and after visiting with her a bit she went up to say hello to Louise.

There were other visitors, Dilara Sabin, phlebotomist and lab technician who works at Kennewick General Hospital along with husband Jack Sabin came in. They are not only neighbors but good friends. Standing next to Dilara above, on the right is Natalie Momotok, nutrition services.

CHAPTER IV: MIXING SCIENCE WITH SPIRITUALITY

Dilara brought an electric swimming tank of fish for Louise. She spent many enjoyable hours watching it. (photo below)

Verdell Ingraham came by as she had done so many times while Louise was at Kadlec and The Life Care Center. Verdell has a bed side manner that always makes smiles on Louise's face when she is near. Verdell was always willing to apply leg and foot massages which Louise really needed. The circulation in her lower limbs was never up to par during the entire ordeal.

Unfortunately I was not always available with a camera when someone stopped by so I did not always get all the photos I would have liked. All the family and friends were concerned when Louise had so quickly disappeared from the Life Care Center. My sister, Lorraine stopped by also.

FROM A PATIENT'S VIEW POINT

It was gratifying to say the least that Louise no longer had any pain in her stomach area. It was the 26th of March and by now she had been in care for almost a month. There were two days at Kennewick General, an operation and 16 days at Kadlec Hospital in Richland, Life Care Center seven days and now back to Kennewick General for two days.

I stayed with Louise everyday during her ordeal, watching her go through trauma with the help of caring hands, medical procedures, spiritually renewed with visits from family and friends and marveling at the visions she had. Her visions only made declarations of what I had already known came her

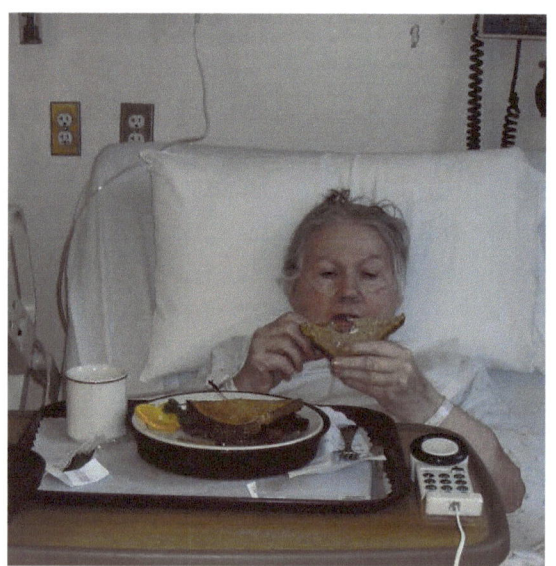

way in her times of need. Others will question but not I for facts were clearly visible of the reality when viewing both what she was seeing and the outcomes as I did.

I smile when I think of Louise eyeing that breakfast toast above on her morning plate. It was as if she was saying, "do I really have to eat this?"

CHAPTER IV: MIXING SCIENCE WITH SPIRITUALITY

There was lots of action around Louise while staff took care of her special needs. Francie Jaynes, MSW, social worker and discharge planner came to talk to Louise (photo below).

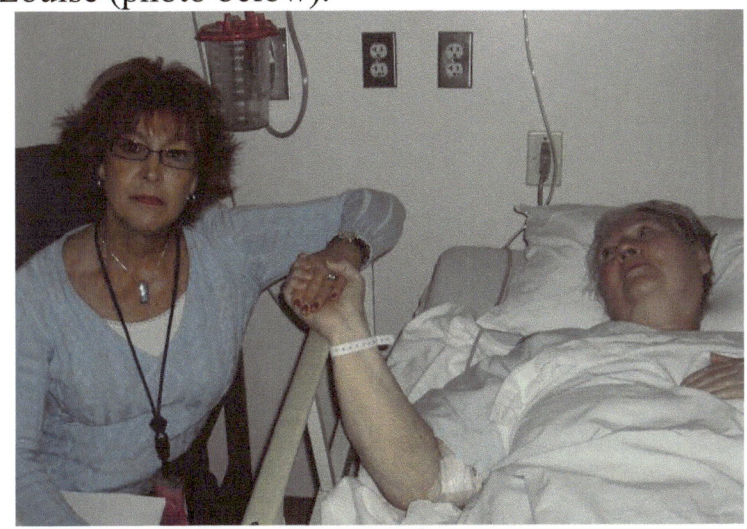

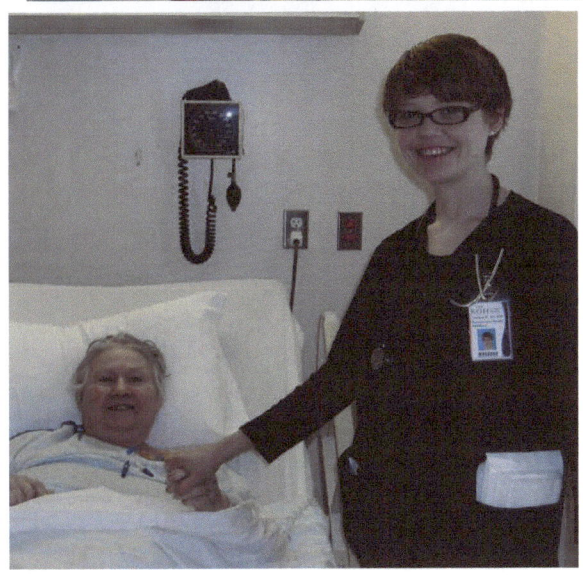

Louise had to be catheterized and Thereasa Witkowski (photo left) came to take care of that (photo left).

Also Kris Benquiat came to take four

vials of blood from her for testing (Kris on the right below).

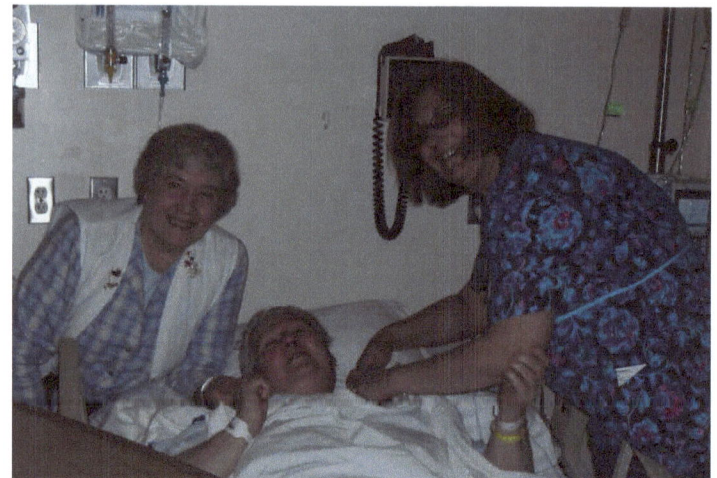

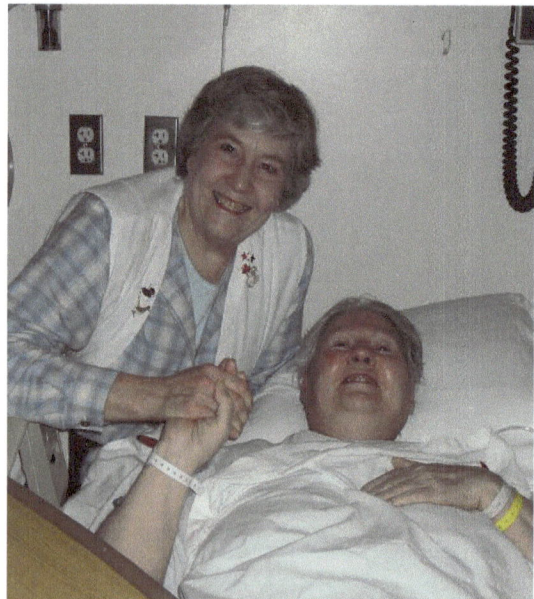

Mary Lamont, physical therapist came in to talk to Louise about her exercise program. Mary's photo is above left and to the left with Louise.

Recuperation was the next road ahead and it too brought its own trials.

CHAPTER V
IN THE GRAND SCHEME OF THINGS

It was March 28th and Dr. Smith, our family doctor visited Louise and I at the Kennewick General Hospital. It was time to discuss rehabilitation for Louise and Dr. Smith gave his medical opinion as to what he determined was the best plan for Louise's complete recovery. He also brought good news that he was cutting the pills down that Louise was to take and he thought with therapy she could go home in about two weeks.

He suggested Louise be transferred to Lady of Lourdes Hospital in Pasco (photo above) to their rehabilitation center instead of going back to Kennewick Life Care Center where they were holding her room for her. Louise and I agreed that by all means if this move to Lady of Lourdes would shorten the time she had to be hospitalized it was the only way to go.

FROM A PATIENT'S VIEW POINT

Dr. Smith put everything into motion and it wasn't long that a transfer bus picked Louise up in her wheel chair and she was on her way to Lady of Lourdes in Pasco. It was a smooth transition and by 5:30 that evening Dr. Donald G Dickens MD, (photo below with Louise) head of the rehabilitation center had been in to examine Louise and assured us that in two weeks or less his team could have her ready to go home.

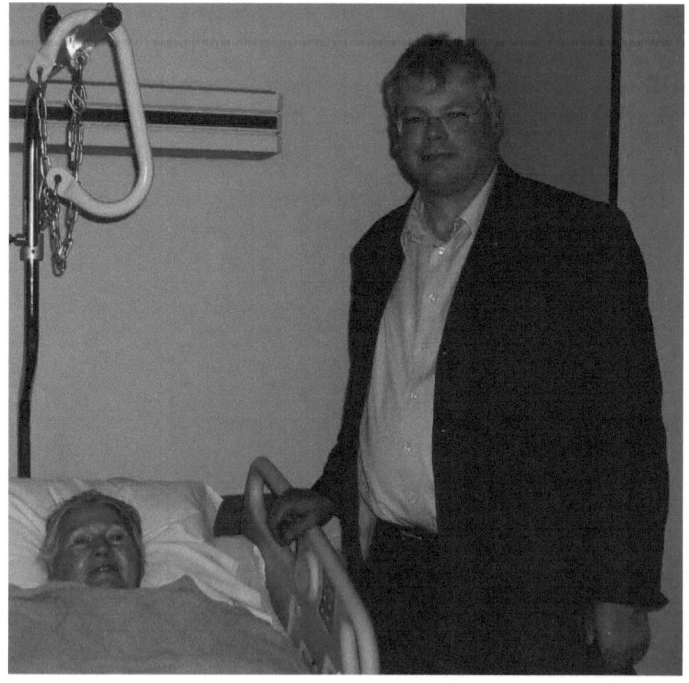

It was comforting to know Louise was in the hands of a team of therapist under Dr. Dickens. He was highly recommended by Dr. Smith and as we found in the days ahead praised by many as supervising the best

CHAPTER V: IN THE GRAND SCHEME OF THINGS

organized team of specialist in the field of inpatient rehabilitation. Each member of his team had their special expertise; they kept daily records and followed up with regular meetings as a group with Dr. Dickens.

Dr. Dickens is one of the most caring doctors I have ever met. He had his regular patient visits at the hospital and came around in between just to checkup. We noted on his days off he still made patient rounds.

The next morning at 7:30 A.M. on March 29th after one night at Lady of Lourdes Hospital the nurses had already removed the catheter from Louise. Still in a wheel chair she took her first visit to the bathroom since she had started her hospital ordeal. It was a welcome start but still Louise had to be catheterized three times a day to remove fluid from the kidneys.

Dr. Dickens stopped by at 8:00 A.M. to see how Louise was doing. When I arrived at 10:00 A.M. a nurse was taking a scan of Louise's stomach to see if all was well due to the long time she had a catheter inserted. Later that day Louise had her first exercise therapy. Each progression for rehabilitation was monitored and recorded. The team members and nurses worked totally together as well as independently caring for Louise.

As the days went by I could see improvement in Louise's ability from sitting up in bed without help to maneuvering herself into the wheel chair and then into the walker. Everyday she was stronger but she still was not eating well. Food did not taste good to her; she was not on a restricted diet so I even tried enticing her with her favorite drink by bringing a tasty latte from the downstairs coffee shop to her room.

From March 3, 2008 to April 3, 2008 I sat by Louise's bedside eight to ten hours every day (Photo of Willard Ingraham above). To pass the time each day besides trying to help her by keeping the glass of water full and cold and anything I could do to see to her small comforts I wrote in my journal each day about the daily happenings and Louise's progress or set backs. I brought my camera and took pictures of the doctors,

CHAPTER V: IN THE GRAND SCHEME OF THINGS

nurses and anyone else that took part in helping her get well.

Louise and I both knew that we would be writing this book "From The Patient's View Point" once she recovered and her full strength returned. I also got permission from every one I took a picture of to use their name and picture in the book. I took over 100 pictures and most of them will be included in this book. The only regret I have is that I was unable to take photos of all the staff that contributed to Louise's recuperation.

The visions Louise had that I have already described were only a few of what was still going on in her mind. She best described the visions as if a video was playing in her head. She said there were some warm spots on each side of her head as if the movie reel was warmed up to play.

I had gotten a list of the medications she was taking from each of the hospitals and there were pills for blood pressure, antibiotics, protein supplement, clonidine, Lasix, Mycelex Troche for yeast infection and pain pills if she needed it for her back. Dr. Smith had eliminated some but there were still lots of medication.

The point is that it is true Louise was full of medication but her visions were marvels in themselves and some take precedence to tell. There was one she kept repeating to me that was running over and over in her head since her surgery. She told me our mail box in front of the house was in danger of being pilfered. I agreed with her but did not think we lived in an area that was as vulnerable as on other streets. She insisted she was seeing thieves in the shadows where pilfering was going on and she was afraid that mail we received on a regular basis from our bank and other sources could easily be taken and dangerous to us if they fell into the wrong hands. I got the point and promised to do something about the mail box later. Louise did not let me forget and kept repeating her vision; it was June before I really had any time to make changes and installed a steel box with a programmed entry built into it.

Our neighbors saw me working on the installation and asked me if I was putting a security box in because of what had happened a few months back. I had not heard so he explained to me that there was a neighbor just a few doors north that had mail stolen. The culprit had canvassed the neighborhood and after mail delivery to a house that was known to have owners away at work, the mail was taken from the box. The credit card numbers on statements were used to order on line and when the packages came the culprit was on hand to pick up the items.

When the home owner finally realized what was going on she reported it then did her own stake out. In a short time she saw the culprit pilfering. From her

CHAPTER V: IN THE GRAND SCHEME OF THINGS

hidden vantage point she took photos of the theft and identifying licenses numbers on the auto. After giving the information to the police it did not take the police long to close in.

Did Louise see these visions as a warning or was it something that was playing in her mind as common sense? You will have to decide; for me it was the miracle of visions as usual with her and another lesson not to ignore revelations.

There were other visions but some really stand out. Louise seemed to be able to see and hear things before they happened. We would be discussing a subject and she would tell me that I had already told her and then she filled in the gaps. This happened frequently and it was easy to see she was revealing information that had not been previously given to her.

On March 31, 2008 Louise was still hospitalized but finally able to walk longer distances and walked out of her room to the nurses' desk with her wheeled walker. It was exhausting for her but with determination she pushed herself to her limits.

On a regular basis the therapists gave her leg and arm exercises also. The circulation in her legs was not what it should be; Louise actually felt pain and a certain amount of numbness in her legs while lying in bed.

FROM A PATIENT'S VIEW POINT

PHOTOS I TOOK OF MANY OF THE STAFF THAT HELPED LOUISE RECUPERATE AT OUR LADY OF LOURDES HOSPITAL, PASCO. WASHINGTON HAS BEEN INSERTED IN THE FOLLOWING PAGES:

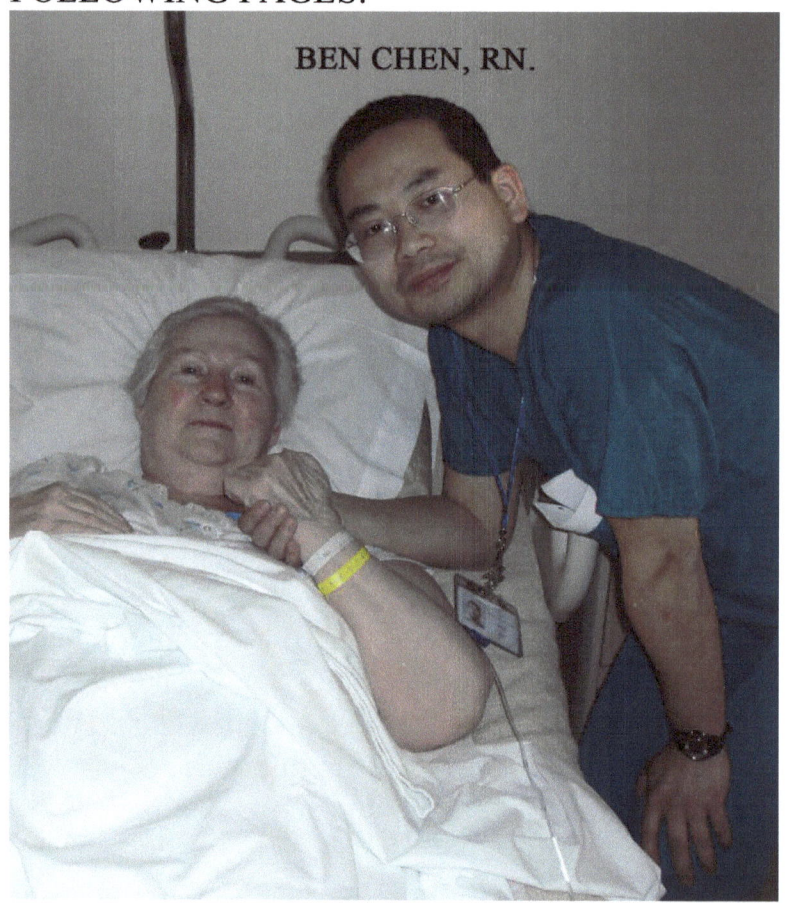

Every day was improvement in Louise's condition but even with the catheter removed Louise still had to have a manual tube to drain her kidneys several times a day. They had given her an MRI and it showed her kidneys now functioning but there was infection in

CHAPTER V: IN THE GRAND SCHEME OF THINGS

her body. At one point at Kadlec she was told if they could not get the kidneys to function she would have to be put on a kidney machine. We were thankful she had passed that milestone and was recuperating even though slowly.

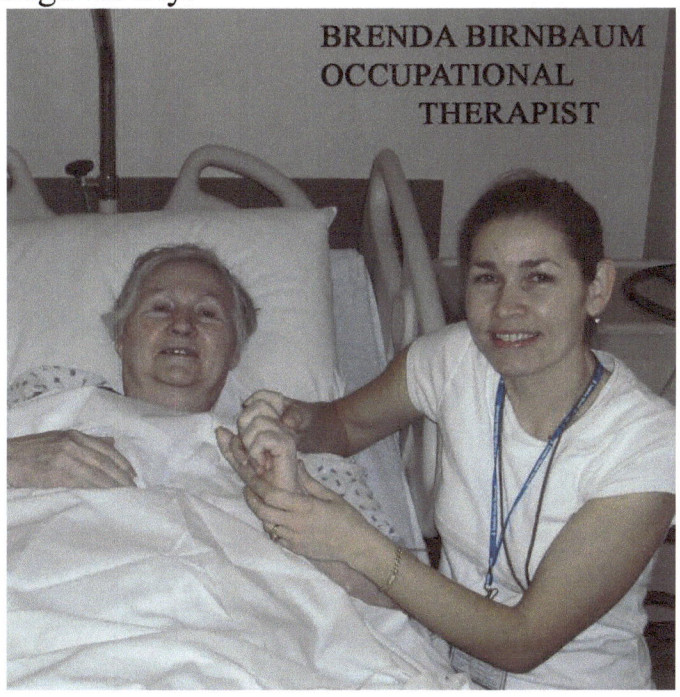

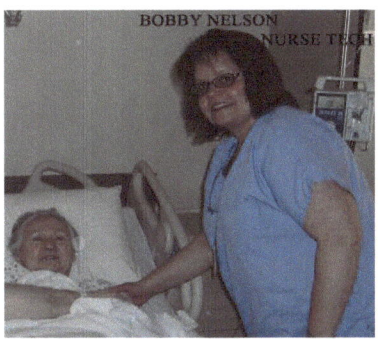

FROM A PATIENT'S VIEW POINT

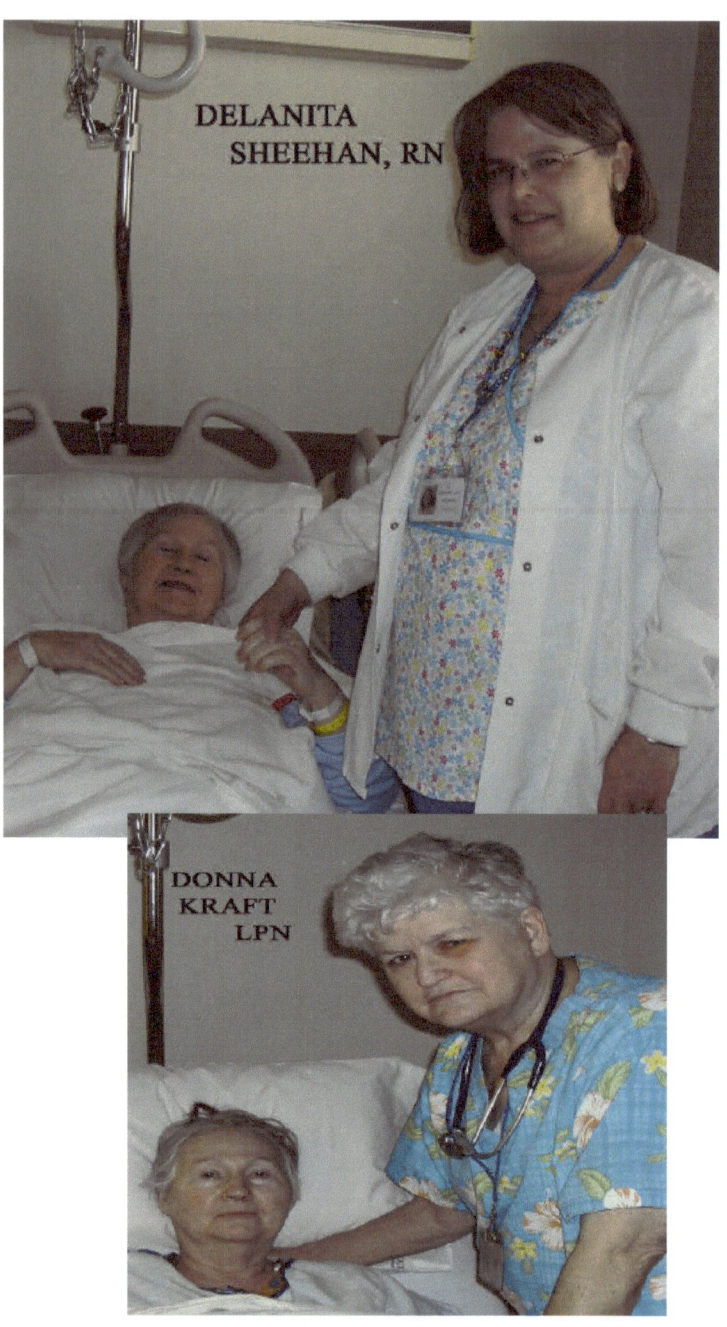

CHAPTER V: IN THE GRAND SCHEME OF THINGS

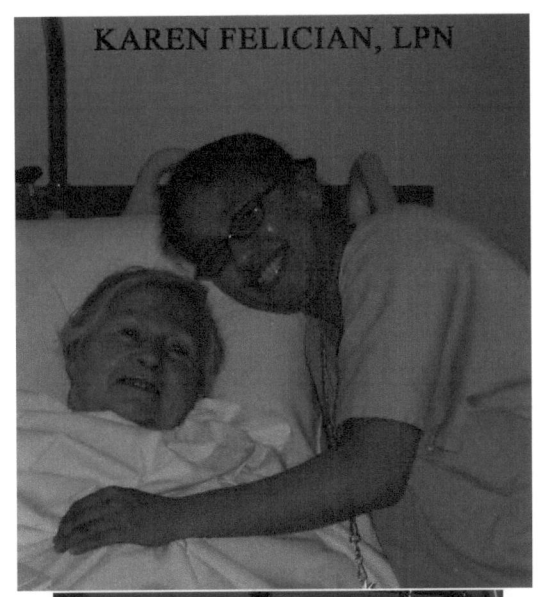

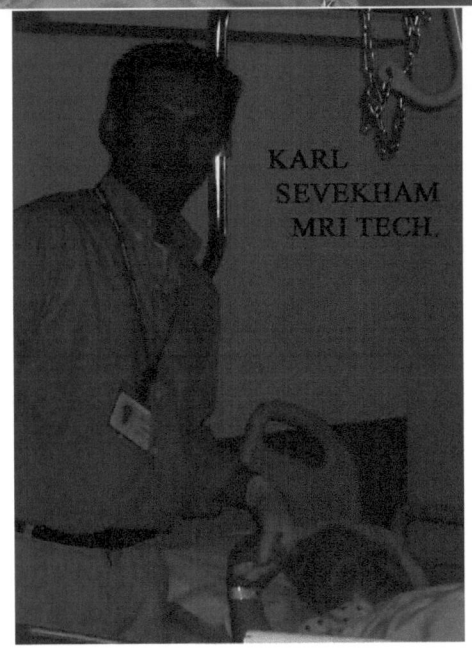

FROM A PATIENT'S VIEW POINT

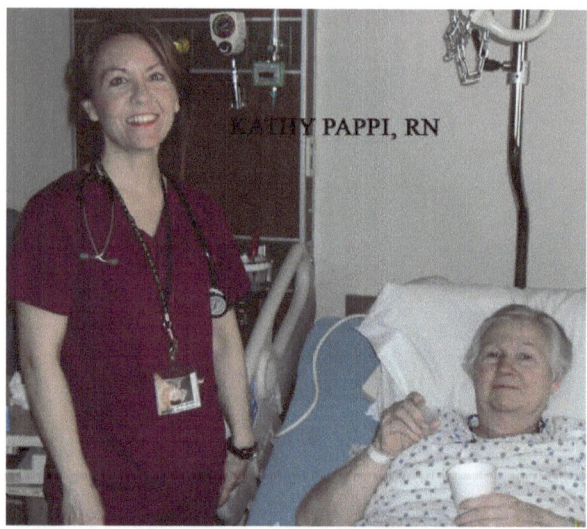

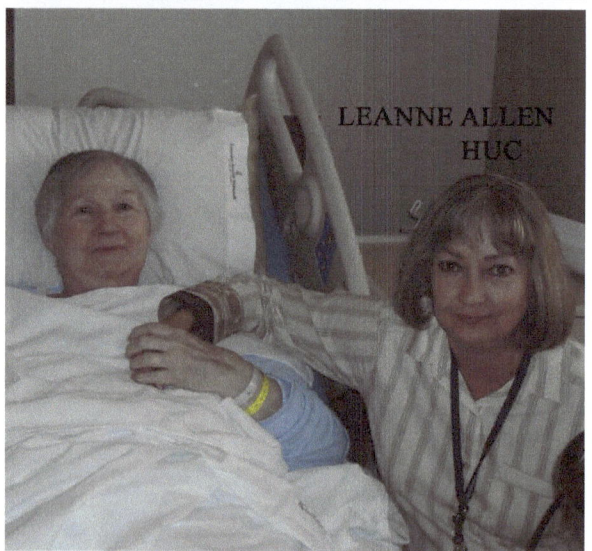

When viewing all of these photos it is evident that each of these professionals are sincere in their giving of kindness and care to their patient. The patient has a smile that says, "I am glad you are here."

CHAPTER V: IN THE GRAND SCHEME OF THINGS

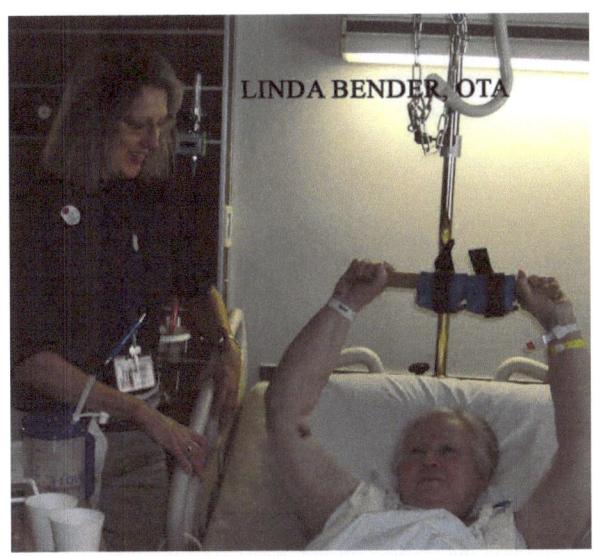

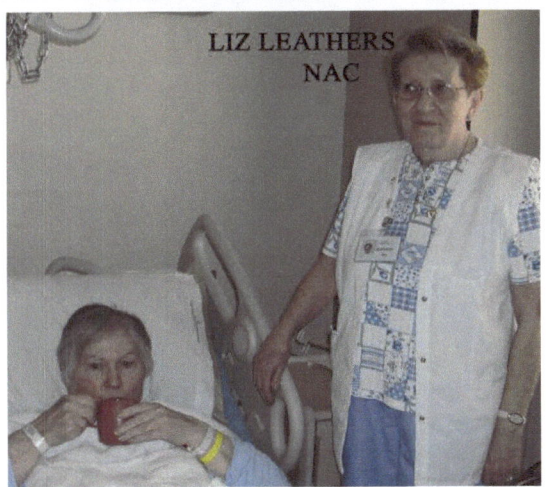

Also in preparation to going home I was given training to catheterize Louise three times a day to empty her bladder as it still was not functioning totally on its own. Also she had regular walking sessions; and finally on the April 2, 2008 she was able

FROM A PATIENT'S VIEW POINT

to walk up and down a twelve step stairway with my help. She was weak and it took all her strength but she also realized until she could manipulate stairs she would not be released to go home.

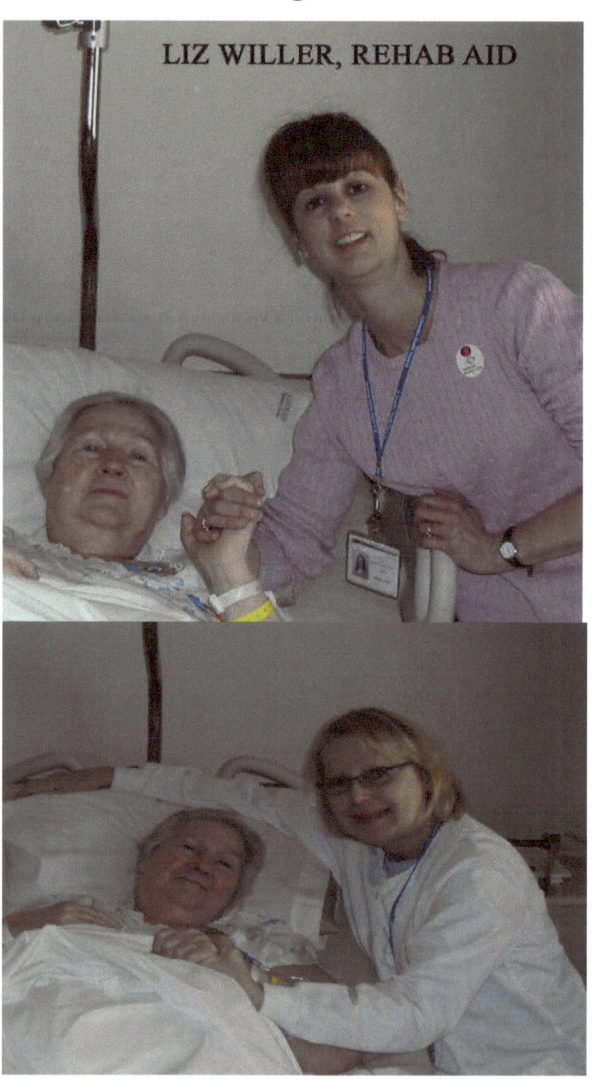

Pam Wilburn, OTRL above right.

CHAPTER V: IN THE GRAND SCHEME OF THINGS

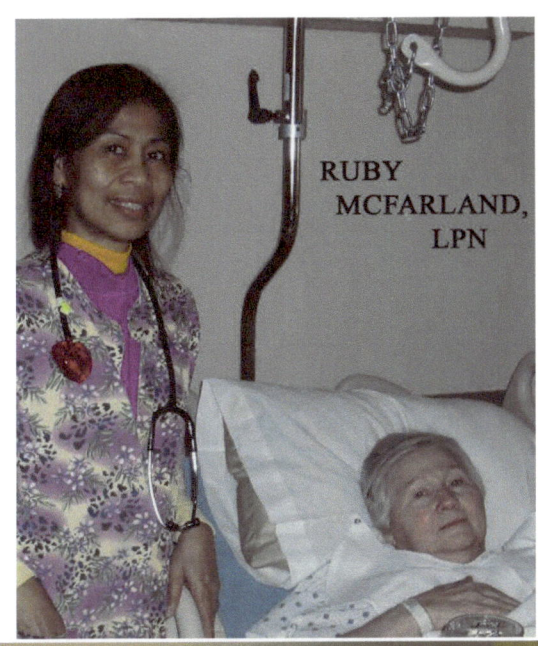

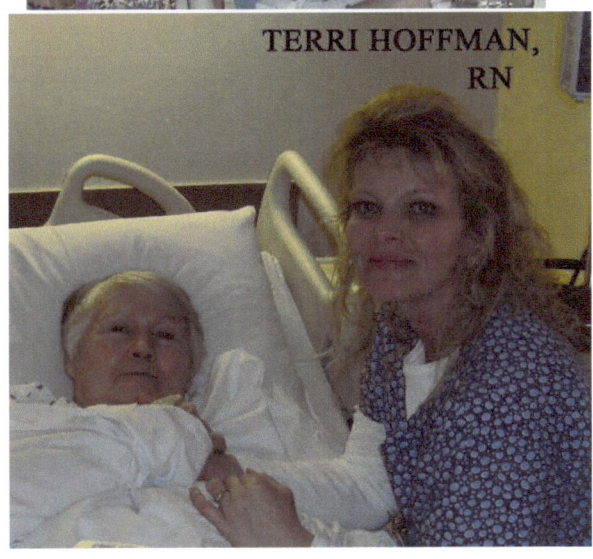

FROM A PATIENT'S VIEW POINT

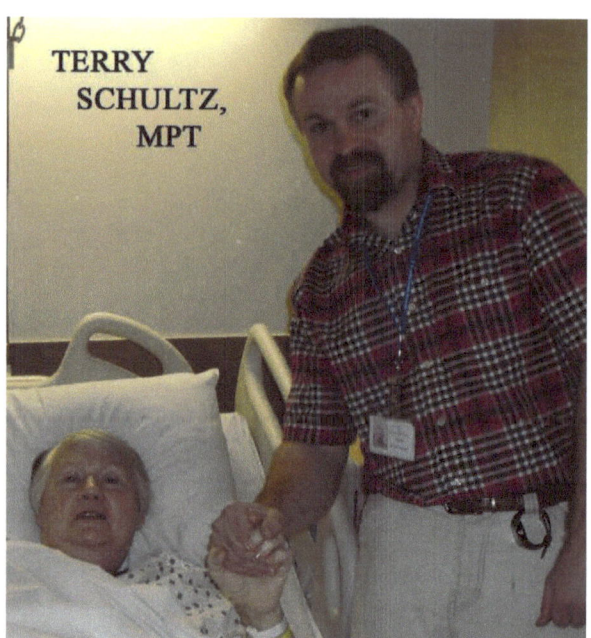

Louise and I discussed how caring everyone was at Lady of Lourdes Hospital. We both agreed it was the best possible place to be for rehabilitation. The care givers were a team of professionals; each took their patient's recovery as a higher standard in measuring their own professional expertise. They deal daily with not only the physical condition of their patients but the patients' depressions and mental attitudes.

I must give recognition to the clergy that visited Louise while confined. Just the fact that she had a one on one with a clergy for prayer was healing; it did not matter if her religious beliefs were different.

CHAPTER V: IN THE GRAND SCHEME OF THINGS

The hospital therapists even took into account how their patients would be cared for when released from the hospital. In preparation for Louise going home I had set up our home entertainment room with more handicap equipment that she needed. There were also stairs she would have to climb daily as the entertainment room I planned to use for her daily care was downstairs from our bedroom.

It was after that last walk with a therapist and the team reporting to Dr. Dickens that he approved a release form and on the 3rd of April Louise was made ready to go home. There were a lot of papers to sign and delays that morning so it was 2:30 P.M. before we finally left the hospital to go home.

It was one month to the day that Louise had entered hospital care. She had been in all three Tri-Cities hospital; Kadlec Hospital, twice in Kennewick General and Lady of Lourdes Hospital as well as at the Kennewick Life Care Center for a week.

Louise settled quickly and happily into home care although she was far from completely well. I had brought her home in a wheel chair; walking only a short distance was all she could manage. Her weakened muscles had to be built up again from the month long stay in bed. I had set the house up with handicap equipment as much as I could. I brought in a special flat hard surface bed so she could do daily bed exercises as she had done at the hospital. It also

FROM A PATIENT'S VIEW POINT

was a necessary place to do the catheterization that needed to be done three times a day.

I was now Louise's full caregiver and my aim was to help her regain her full health back. In the grand scheme of things, at this time, as one would say, medicine, therapy, lots of tender love and prayers would be the answer to achieving the desired results.

I was so happy to have Louise home with me again. I knew that I would be up to the task to help her get well with complete recovery.

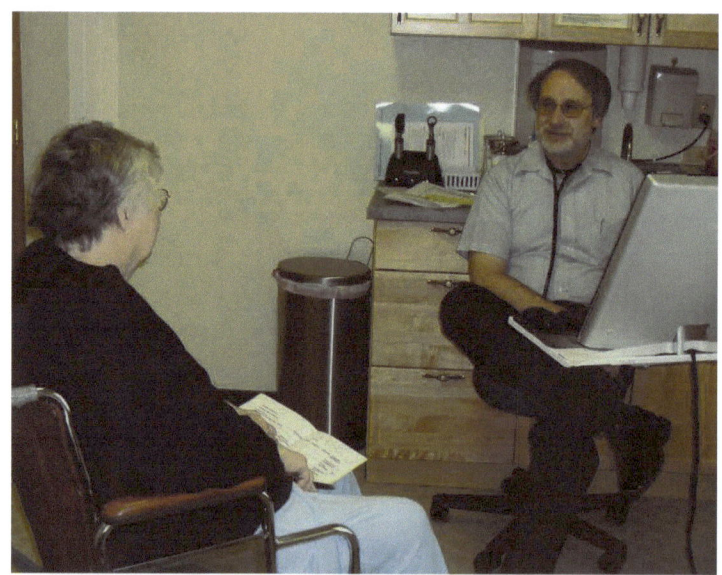

On April 15, 2008 Louise had an appointment with Dr. Matt Smith at his office in Kennewick. Above is a photo of Dr. Smith talking to Louise and taking notes on his computer.

CHAPTER V: IN THE GRAND SCHEME OF THINGS

This was the first outing Louise had since returning home. Although she was still wheel chair bound except for short walks I could see her regaining strength in her legs everyday from short walks she was taking at home. She kept telling me that the trip up and down the stairs each day was the best possible therapy to building leg muscles.

Louise had her work cut out for her. She was now eating better but not as well as I thought she should. I could see that gaining her full strength back was going to take a long time. I was convinced she would fully recover.

FROM A PATIENT'S VIEW POINT

CHAPTER VI
    A NEW BEGINNING

For me, Louise, it was truly a new beginning. Home at last; it had seemed like such a faraway place from my vantage point from a hospital setting. I knew I was fortunate to be able to leave the hospital when I did and hopeful I would regain all my strength back to carry on in a manner I was accustomed to. I was humbled by what had happened to me. I knew it was serious and could have had a far worse outcome. I also knew that my experiences were nothing compared to traumatic issues so many others have faced in their lives.

Willard was now my full time caregiver. He had the stamina and strength needed to give me the 24-7 care I needed. He has always had a positive outlook. How well we all know the importance of having the closeness of someone that no matter what happens we can count on them to always be there helping and encouraging. Willard was and is that person in my life. Now it was up to me to follow his lead and no matter how I felt to continue building my strength.

I needed objects to hang on to for walking in the house as the walker did not go through the doors easily. Willard put up hand bars in the bathroom and even a place to sit on a stool in the shower. Things for the handicapped that I had never dreamed I would have to use or even thought about in the way that I needed them now. There were times I was angry at myself because I wasn't progressing as fast as I thought I should but I never gave up and in time my strength did come back.

I have to speak of the generosity of the Catholic Church's help program that offers equipment to the handicapped. It was through them that we had, on loan, built up toilet seats, a seat to sit on for the shower and a wheel chair. They never asked my church affiliation; their organization was there to help anyone in need. It saved us a great deal of money and we were grateful for the service they provided. I did not realize how important a public service of this magnitude was until I was the needy.

I was scheduled to have out-patient therapy three times a week at Kennewick General. My first appointment left doubts if I was strong enough to continue therapy. I could manage some of the easier exercise equipment but there were some bicycle types that gave me excruciating pain in the sciatic nerve area of my back and down into my legs. That night I got very little sleep. My back and legs not only ached but gave me endless pain. I tried another therapy session and the same thing happened; it was then I knew I had started a therapy that was too difficult for me just yet. After a few days of rest I went back to bed exercises that I had been taught to do in the hospital.

CHAPTER VI: A NEW BEGINNING

I grew stronger as the weeks went by. Willard took me shopping to get me out of the house and at first it was in a wheel chair, then I graduated to a walker with a seat to sit down on when I was exhausted. It was a strange feeling to be looking at the direction I needed to walk as on a path and not be able to walk a straight line. My equilibrium was faulty. Finally I could walk by hanging onto the grocery cart that Willard wheeled along. After months I got enough strength I could go it alone. Eventually I learned to use a walking stick and walked in our back yard for exercise without assistance.

I tried to keep my mind busy with reading and finally was strong enough that I could sit at the computer for short periods of time to work on graphics that I love.

It was also at the computer that I asked my many questions of the entities I believe surround me at all times. This phenomenon of asking a question and then listen for an answer has been with me as long as I can remember. I have always used the question and answer as a way to receive information on a need to know basis.

While I was hospitalized vision after vision came to me without asking but I realize I had a need to know from what I saw and heard. Some of you reading this will believe it was the medication talking; maybe but on the other hand I still know what I saw and heard.

FROM A PATIENT'S VIEW POINT

I still had warm spots on each side of my head when I came home from the hospital but my mind never failed the energy tests and questions I asked. I could work the mind as I always had by concentrating on a desire to know the answer, then ask a question in thought and listen as I typed the answers.

The only way I know how to explain this phenomenon is and was as if the energy forces within my mind can and do reach out to energy forces around me. It is like two electrical currents connecting and electromagnetism carries answers to me through thoughts that I could and can then either pen or type.

Ok; I am not a scientist but if I can do this and it helps me find answers then I believe it is possible for all others to do the same if they desire. I tell myself why not use this gift I have to help others learn the process and they too can find answers for their needs.

I remember the days when I was ridiculed for my visions. It is still difficult to be open and allow others to see into my own darkness where the energies flow. Thank goodness with new scientific findings the public is more open minded than before but there will always be the doubters. Can I handle this? I can if in my own mind I believe what I see and hear is factual and I do.

The scientific experiments reported today are with more open minds to finding more marvels. I am but a

CHAPTER VI: A NEW BEGINNING

small particle in the sand but perhaps my experience with visions and questions will entice others to try it with the hope of finding needed answers. My life is not over and as surely as I can still write and can have a voice I will continue to offer my own insights.

I realize that individuals may find the entrance to this unique world of energy in different manners. There is nothing unusual about that. If you are interested then for a moment just concentrate on knowing and believing we have energy forces around us, within us and out into space. Use a single simple question with your mind, and then concentrate on listening for an answer. With practice this process can open the door to receiving messages.

For my purpose, having experienced the thought process I described, I like to concentrate on a subject and after receiving an answer continue asking questions on the same subject. In this way I can thoroughly cover a subject until I have all the answers I need. It only works when I am rested and have a quiet time to simply ask and quietly listen for the answer. It is as simple as that.

Through my ordeal and recovery I had my times when I doubted I could overcome a physical handicap. Not being able to walk was one of those things that really bothered me. The stairs I went up and down in our home helped build up the leg muscles as did the other exercises and I had the determination but not being

FROM A PATIENT'S VIEW POINT

able to walk a straight path really upset me. I did not know how to even begin overcoming poor equilibrium. Those were times that my visions and thoughts helped me cope. I asked questions about my lack of ability and I was always given answers that set me on a positive way of thinking. Sometimes it was answers like "just keep trying, it will come."

I only mean to be sharing my inner thoughts and philosophy not convincing anyone of my abilities. For you believers don't get excited; those answers to winning the lottery are not going to come. It is only questions that meet the need for growth of the soul for that individual or others that will be answered.

CHAPTER VII
MY VIEW POINT

My view point as a patient is my own and is my opinion alone. I can not cover all the fields of care but I can report on my own. As I write of my views it comes from my own observations in the areas that I was cared for.

I will start with my hospital care. I came home from the hospital in a wheel chair. Could or should I have gotten better hospital treatment? I believe I had the finest doctors and hospital staff in the business of caring for others. The doctors were specialists in their fields and in my case their medical expertise was what I needed to find and treat my health problems.

Not one nurse, staff, therapist or caregiver was ever unprofessional in my treatment; they were all caring and dedicated. No matter what their day might have been like when they entered my room they had one thing in mind; total care for the patient.

There were times that I realized there were shortages of nurses on duty. I was told it was because there is not enough entering the field of medicine due to financing an education. A problem I hope will be addressed nation wide with providing funding through loans and scholarships for aspiring students to enter the field of their choice.

FROM A PATIENT'S VIEW POINT

I see too many students struggling to cover college expenses with outside jobs while attending college full time. We owe it to our younger generation to do better thus allowing full attention to the education of choice. Not only that but the field of nursing is huge and covers a multitude of needs; all in the end helping all of us with our personal health issues.

I found the technicians, dieticians and other staff all supportive in care for their patients. I had infection through out my body and an infected growth that was removed from my back. There was pneumonia to overcome as well as two bleeding ulcers. At one point I was bleeding from the nose and mouth and was rushed from the Life Care Center where I had been placed to recuperate to emergency care at the hospital where they pumped my stomach that had filled with blood from the bleeding ulcers. The aftermath included giving me blood transfusions.

I am not judging anyone for the series of problems I had after entering hospital care. I understand that the problems were manifested by other underlying problems where one led to yet another problem. The infections that were in my body when I was admitted to the hospital did a good job of taking over other vital functions in the body. My kidneys were not functioning properly as was other vital organs and I had a high fever. The special care I got dealt with each problem quickly and in a professional manner.

CHAPTER VII: MY VIEW POINT

I did not know what was going on outside of my room except on how it affected me personally but I did see there were caring hands all around me and team work. Would I ask for anything to have changed? Not on the medical care side from my view point. I was in three different hospitals and a life care center and only saw what was happening to me that I can report on. In some cases I was too sick to realize the total consequences of my problems at the time.

Afterward though when I was home and the bills came in I did definitely see where improvements could be made in how a patient is charged. I was a patient covered with Medicare and had secondary insurance. I was fortunate; if not for the insurance coverage my financial situation could have been desperate. In reviewing costs though I had and have concerns about some of the charges.

Yes, I was lucky in that Medicare covered 80% and my secondary insurance covered the other 20% but this did not mean the charges themselves didn't raise questions. I was a patient and in no condition to monitor what was involved in the costs of my care on a daily basis. I received no itemized list of the charges from the hospitals or life-care center. I truly believe complete transparency in how the costs were charged should have been furnished to me as a patient and for family review.

FROM A PATIENT'S VIEW POINT

Was it the responsibility of the care center to furnish the patient itemized breakdowns?

I received, in the mail, after I got home from the hospital disclosure statements from Medicare and my secondary insurance. They contained no total itemization; there was only an overview of costs. To further explain to those not familiar with Medicare procedure, the costs presented were neither itemized nor specific.

I do know that all providers are given a list of health care procedures from Medicare and allowable charges for payment. This list of items shows the dollar amount allowed by Medicare and includes a code number referencing that type of charge. From this list the provider uses these codes to then charge Medicare.

I would expect to be told that by coding charges it saves time and money both for the provider and Medicare. I say we are a computer age that has the ability to transfer the basic information via internet to all parties including the patient for transparency. Those that are in the business of inputting charges wherever initiated certainly have a record keeping process that could be passed on for patient auditing purposes.

CHAPTER VII: MY VIEW POINT

I had no idea as to the details of supplies or additional costs for medications or oxygen and other care items etc that were used for my benefit.

I can not say that I was overcharged on the billings because of lack of details but I do see costs rising. I am the patient and why wouldn't I want to have a break down of costs and an opportunity for complete review of all charges? I then can ask for answers to any question and concerns I may have.

Tracking and auditing Medicare procedures needs an overhaul. Included should be a misdemeanor of a provider knowingly trying to up the cost by how the codes are presented to Medicare.

The scary part for the patients are if the costing allowable by Medicare to providers is not fair there will be fewer providers accepting Medicare patients and that would take a drastic toll on the seniors and others depending on Medicare coverage. Another auditing and pricing system needs to be installed with periodic updates and reviews.

Another need is the posting of a patient's records pertaining to history of that patient's health events. Why not have the patient's history on the internet to only be accessed by the patient's doctors by a code for privacy. It would cut down on repeats of tests and give the doctors a better history of the patient before administering and prescribing medications.

FROM A PATIENT'S VIEW POINT

I had pneumonia during my stay in the hospital which added to my already serious problems. Could it have been prevented? I don't know, probably not. Medically I realize an individual's overall health does lend itself to further problems. Having said that the patient's health is a factor I ask, what is wrong with research on care and medical procedures for changes and initiating new ways for prevention?

Another big question I have is how can there be better ways of tracking the medication a patient is taking? At one point I was given 7 or 8 total medications at the same time; all were prescriptions and some from different doctors. I had family that went on line to the web site for Mayo Clinic to check for side effects from the medications I was taking. They found there were side effects for potential bleeding ulcers. I may have had ulcers previously that I did not know about but if my history had been available would I have been prescribed with some of these medications? Again, I don't know but I believe it is another area that needs to be looked into by professionals in the business of prescribing medicine.

From my view point, I want to see more preventive measures taken. I don't know where or how I got the infection that led to a growth on my spine. Was I careless in someway; I don't know. If I was better informed on what and where such problems as mine come from could and would I have been in a better

CHAPTER VII: MY VIEW POINT

position to maintain a healthy body? It may have not made any difference in my case but knowing more may have. Maybe I would have recognized I had an infection in my body and instead I thought it was old age creeping in.

A long time ago I had a DNC in a hospital that costs were covered by Medicare. I later got a report showing how much the hospital was allowed for the procedure and how much the hospital charged over the allowable amount. I knew Medicare was billed using codes to identify the procedure so I asked accounting why they submitted a charge to Medicare for more than they knew the procedure would cost. I was told that it was done to get Medicare to readjust the scale and increase the allowable amount.

Fairness in covering costs as well as how services are rendered is all important and needs oversight. None the less we are all in this together and if our insurance protection plans had more preventive care coverage I am positive there would be less serious outcomes. From a lay persons view point I can certainly understand the difference of regular checkups and follow up of preventive care than is available now. After all we all want quality of life.

One last thing; in my case I had my husband Willard to give information needed to my care givers and to monitor my daily care. I was too sick to do it myself. I understand some hospitals are now using an authorized patient communicator listed at the time of patient's admittance to the hospital. I urge all hospitals and care centers to follow suit. In many cases the patient is unable to deal with it themselves. I say, "all patients need an overseer."

I was a patient and my view point is from a lay persons view but aren't most patients knowledge outside of the medical profession minimal? I am one of the lucky ones in that I have regained most of my health. I only offer my opinions to others and am hopeful my story and visions inspire others to look within for answers.

CHAPTER VII: MY VIEW POINT

www.ingramcontent.com/pod-product-compliance
Lightning Source LLC
Chambersburg PA
CBHW042007150426
43195CB00002B/47